The Canadian's Guide to Starting a Small Business

by Andrew Dagys, CPA, CMA,
Margaret Kerr, and JoAnn Kurtz

WILEY

Publisher's Acknowledgments

Authors: Andrew Dagys, CPA, CMA, Margaret Kerr, and JoAnn Kurtz

Senior Acquisitions Editor: Tracy Boggier

Project Editor: Elizabeth Kuball

Compilation Editor: Georgette Beatty

Production Editor: Mohammed Zafar Ali

Cover Photo: © mightyisland/ Getty Images, © stockish/ Shutterstock

The Canadian's Guide to Starting a Small Business

Published by John Wiley & Sons, Inc.
111 River St.
Hoboken, NJ 07030-5774
http://www.wiley.com

Copyright © 2019 by John Wiley & Sons, Inc., Hoboken, New Jersey

For general information on our other products and services, please contact our Business Development Department in the U.S. at 317-572-3205.

Library of Congress Control Number: 2019942829

ISBN 978-1-119-60926-1 (pbk)

Manufactured in the United States of America

V10011104_061319

Table of Contents

1

Do You Have the
Right Stuff?

So, you're thinking of starting your own business. Every year, lots of Canadians of all ages and backgrounds get the entrepreneurial urge and take the leap to start businesses. Some of those businesses become very successful, and some of them fail.

Business success or failure isn't the result of fate or random chance. A business does well for good reasons — like providing a great product or service, having a solid marketing plan, and having an owner with good management skills.

Likewise, when a business goes under, you can often identify the reasons — lack of money to get properly started, poor timing or location for entering the market, or a wipeout on the customer service front. Whatever the reason for a business failure, it usually boils down to this: The business owner didn't look carefully before leaping into a new business frontier.

This chapter and the others in this book help you think about going into business before you hit the ignition button and blast off. Think of this first chapter as "countdown."

The Pros and Cons of Small Business Ownership

People start up their own businesses for different reasons. One of the best reasons is that they've found a business opportunity and idea that are just too attractive to pass up. A good reason is that they want to work for themselves rather than for someone else. A discouraging — but still valid — reason is that their other job options are poor (the number of small business start-ups always rises when the economy sinks or stinks).

Whatever your reason is for wanting to become an entrepreneur, you should know that life as an entrepreneur is a bit of a mixed bag. Don't say you weren't warned. Running your own business has some great advantages, but it also has its share of disadvantages.

The pros

Here are some of the good things about going into business for yourself:

- **You're free.** You'll have the freedom to make your own decisions — you're in charge now. Only investors, customers and clients, government regulators, and so on will tell you what to do.

  You'll have the freedom to choose your own work hours — in theory, anyway. You may not be able to get away with sleeping in until noon or concentrating your productive hours around 3 a.m. But you're more likely to be able to pick up the kids from school at 3 p.m., or exercise from 10 a.m. to 11 a.m., or grocery shop during normal office hours.

  You'll have the freedom to create your own work environment — surround yourself with dirty coffee cups and empty candy wrappers if you feel like it.

- **You can be creative.** You can build your business from scratch following your own ideas rather than following someone else's master plan.

- **You'll face new challenges.** Every day. And twice as many on days that end in a *y*. You'll never be able to say that work is always the same old boring routine.

- **Your job will be secure . . . as long as you have a business.** Your business may fail — but no one can fire you. You can ask yourself to resign, though.

- **You'll have increased financial opportunities.** If your business is successful, you have the potential to make more than you can as an employee.

- **You'll have tax advantages.** This is especially true if your business is not incorporated (a sole proprietorship or a partnership), but it's also true in a different way if your business is incorporated (see Chapter 7).

The cons

Bet the previous section got you all enthused and excited about entrepreneurship. But calm down for a minute — being an entrepreneur has plenty of disadvantages, too. For some people, they outweigh the advantages. For example:

- **You may not make a lot of money.** You may make enough money to live on, but it may not come in regularly like an employment paycheque, so you'll have cash flow predictability and budgeting problems. Or you may not make enough money to live on. You may not even make any money at all. You may go bankrupt and lose not only your business, but most of your personal possessions as well.

- **You lose easy and inexpensive access to employment benefits if you don't hang on to employment elsewhere.** These may be benefits that you have come to count on — extended health and dental benefits, disability insurance, life insurance, a pension plan, and so on.

- **You'll have to work really hard.** That is, if you want to succeed — and you won't just be working at the business your business is about. You'll also have to do stuff you may not be trained to do, such as accounting, sales, and collection work.

- **You may not have a lot of free time.** You may see less of your friends, family, and pets (even if you're working at home) and have less time for your favourite activities. Getting a business up and running takes more than hard work; it also takes your time and commitment. Don't scoff that you won't let that happen to you, at least not until you've put in hours filling out government paperwork on a beautiful sunny day that would be perfect for, well, almost anything else. By the way, you don't get paid for your sacrificed time, either.

- **You may have to put a lot of your own money into starting up the business.** And even if you can borrow the money, unless the lender is The Bank of Mom and

Dad, you'll have to give personal guarantees that the money will be repaid (with interest) within a certain time. The pressure is building. (For more on borrowing, see Chapter 5.)

By the way, not to add to the pressure or anything, but you should know that you might lose your own money or not be able to repay borrowed money because of factors beyond your control. You could get sick (and now you probably don't have disability insurance), be flattened by a competitor, squashed by a nose-diving economy, or whacked by a partner who pulls out on you.

- **You are the bottom line.** No excuses — success is up to you, and failure is your fault. You'll have to keep on top of changes in your field, the impact of new technology, economic fluctuations. . . .

- **Your personal life can stick its nose into your business life in a major way.** If you and your spouse split up, your spouse may be able to claim a share of your business under equalization provisions in the family law of some provinces. You might have to sell your home, your business, or your business assets (business property) to pay off your spouse.

How to Know If You Have the Small Business Personality

Whatever your reason for wanting to go into business for yourself, and whatever the business you decide to go into, stop and check whether you have the right personality for the adventure before you start. This is true whether you really want to go into business for yourself or whether you think you have no choice but to do so. And it will give you an excuse to put off figuring out your finances.

Realizing that you don't have the right stuff to run your own business is better done before you sink a lot of time and effort, and maybe even money, into a business. You can always pursue other options.

And if you find you're not going to be the perfect entrepreneur, but you're determined to go ahead anyway, then a self-assessment will tell you where your weaknesses lie and show you where you need to improve or get outside help.

An entrepreneur needs most of the following qualities — whether you were born with them, or developed them, or are about to get working on them now:

- **Self-confidence:** You have to believe in yourself and your abilities . . . no matter what other people might think. You have to believe that your success depends on the good work you know you can do and not on matters beyond your control. However, your self-confidence should be realistic and not induced by whatever weird thing they put in the coffee at your current workplace.

- **Goal orientation:** You have to know what you want, whether it's to revolutionize a particular industry or to be home when your children return from school. However, if your main goals are money, power, and prestige, you probably need to reorient yourself toward something a little more attainable in the small business sector.

- **Drive to be your own boss:** The burning desire and the ability to be your own boss — if you need or even want direction about what to do next, you won't make it in your own business. You have to be able to make your own plans and carry them out.

- **Independence:** The ability to work independently rather than as part of a team. You've probably had propaganda pounded into your head since you were a kid that teamwork is really important, and maybe even better than working on your own. It isn't if you're an entrepreneur.

- **Survival skills:** The ability to survive without a social group is handy. When you start up your own business, you'll probably be working by yourself for some time. If you need people around you to chat with, or else you start to go crazy . . . then you may go crazy.

- **People skills:** Even though you have to be able to get along without being surrounded by people all the time, you still have to get along with people. You'll be dealing directly with customers and clients, investors, suppliers, associates, and employees, and you need their willing cooperation.

- **Determination and persistence:** You have to want to succeed, and you have to plan to succeed and keep working at succeeding. It's that "fire in the belly" stuff you hear about from people who look like they haven't slept in the past eight months.

- **Self-discipline:** You can't let yourself be distracted from your work by nice weather, phone calls from family and friends, earthquakes, or wrestling matches on TV.

- **Reliability:** You'll build most of your important business relationships by always meaning what you say and doing what you promise.

- **Versatility:** You have to be prepared to do many different things in short periods of time, probably constantly switching from task to task.

- **Creativity:** You have to want to do something new or something old in a new way. If copying what someone else is already doing is the best you can manage, you may not go far.

- **Resourcefulness:** Creativity's country cousin, resourcefulness, means being prepared to try different ways of doing things if the first way doesn't work.

- **Organizational talents:** You'll be plunged into chaos if you can't organize your goals, your time, or your accounts, to name just a few things.

- **Risk management instincts:** You have to be able to spot risks, weigh them, and come up with a plan to steer around them or soften their impact in case of a collision. (See Chapter 7 for some help in managing risk.)

- **Nerves of steel in a crisis:** Nerves of granite, titanium, oak, and so on are acceptable. Nerves of rubber, talc, or pasta al dente are not. Crises won't necessarily be frequent, but they will occur. Don't count on gin or prescription drugs to stiffen your spine during a crisis. And you can't collapse until the crisis is over.

- **Pick-yourself-up-itiveness — a combination of optimism and grit:** You're going to have failures, some of them caused by your own mistakes, and you have to see failures as valuable experiences rather than as signs that you and your business are doomed.

- **Opportunism:** You need to not only recognize opportunities when they come along, but also seek them out — and even create them yourself.

- **Success management instincts:** You can't let yourself be bowled over or lulled by success. You have to be able to see each success as a platform on which you can build your next success.

- **Objectivity:** For a business owner, it's always reality-check time. You have to have the courage to stare down reality's throat and acknowledge your own mistakes. You also have to corner reality by getting feedback about your business and how you run it from customers and clients, suppliers, professional advisors, competitors, employees, and even your mother-in-law. Then you have to have the strength to make necessary changes.

That's a long list. And you'll also need a Zen-like calm about not having a regular paycheque. Not only will you not get a bank deposit once a month, but you won't get paid for sick days, personal days off, or days when you show up at the office but are too zonked to work.

In addition, it helps if your parents (or close relatives or close friends) are or were in business for themselves. You may have absorbed some business know-how from them; plus, you may have easy access to advice.

And to finish you off, good health and physical stamina can do an entrepreneur no harm.

A great free resource is the online entrepreneurial assessment provided by the Business Development Bank of Canada. Go to www.bdc.ca and search for *Entrepreneurial Potential Self-Assessment* using the Search tool in the upper-right corner. If that doesn't work, hover your mouse over Articles and Tools, and click Entrepreneur's Toolkit; from there, click the Entrepreneurial Potential Self-Assessment link. This robust questionnaire includes 50 statements that will take you about 15 minutes to thoughtfully complete. The questions are not binary — there is no right or wrong answer. All the tool requires is your honest response. When you finish the questionnaire, your answers are summarized in a way that helps you to self-assess your entrepreneurial traits, motivations, aptitudes, and attitudes.

Other Factors to Consider Before Starting Your Business

Even if you're a potential paragon of entrepreneurship, think about the following before leaping into business for yourself:

- Would your personal life allow you to take the entrepreneurial plunge right now?
- Do you have the practical resources to go into the particular business you have your heart set on?
- Is this a good time (for economic and market reasons) for anyone to go into this particular business?

Your personal life

What's going on in your personal life right now? Starting a small business makes more sense at some times than at others. Think about the following questions:

- Do you need a steady income right now — maybe because you have small children and your spouse has given up paid employment to stay home with them, or because you have debts to repay?
- Do you need a steady and conventional lifestyle right now because all hell is breaking loose in the rest of your life?
- Do you need to be physically present in your home more (maybe because you want to spend time with your young children after school or you have to look after an elderly parent), so a home-based business makes more sense than working outside your home?

- Do you have some money to throw around right now, perhaps from an inheritance or a buyout package from your employer?
- Would you have trouble raising the necessary cash to start a business — say, because you've just gone bankrupt?

 If you have a spouse, or someone who depends on your income or companionship, ask him or her to list the pros and cons of your going into business for yourself right now — from his or her own point of view. You might as well get it all out in the open.

Your practical resources

Do you really have what it takes to start this business? Ask yourself now, before you invest time, money, and effort and maybe pass up other work or opportunities for which you're better suited.

For starters, if you go into any business, you'll have to

- Find customers, identify customer needs, develop new product and service ideas, decide on prices, and develop promotional strategies (see Chapter 8).
- Persuade customers to buy.
- Do good work so customers will (a) be more likely to pay you and (b) come back to you.

- Enter into contracts to buy and provide goods and services — you need to know what has to go into the contract, even if you don't draft it yourself.

- Have a working knowledge of the law so you don't break it and it doesn't break you (for example, you need to know about different kinds of taxes and levies), non-discrimination in providing goods and services or in hiring, breach of the Competition Act in your advertising, and arrest of shoplifters. (You can read more about the Competition Act, which has to do with the regulation of trade and commerce, at `https://laws-lois.justice.gc.ca/eng/acts/C-34/index.html`.)

- Understand the financial side of your business and keep proper accounts (payable and receivable), collect and pay taxes, borrow money, manage cash flow, handle credit, and create and stick to a budget.

- Keep track of the product or service you provide or sell (if it's a service, you provide your time) and purchase supplies and materials on time.

- Buy and use a computer and software.

- Get money owed to you by deadbeat customers and clients.

- Eventually hire, supervise, train, motivate, and evaluate employees.

If you don't have these skills, you'll have to fill in the blanks. You can find some ideas about that in Chapter 2. (Don't get into a funk. You may be surprised at how many of the skills you've already acquired through courses at school, jobs you've held, participation in clubs or organizations, and even just from running your own life.)

You'll also need a set of skills to run the particular kind of business you have in mind. Ask yourself these questions:

- **Do I need particular skills, talents, years of experience, expertise, or connections to succeed in this business?** Or, in some cases, do I need all this just to get my foot in the door of this business?

- **Is this business heavily regulated?** Do I need particular education, training, or other official qualifications before I start? Do I need government approval that may not be automatic?

- **Is this business expensive?** Do I need a lot of money to get set up? (For example, will it cost a lot to develop the product or service, to manufacture the product, or to find customers or develop a distribution system?)

If you don't know the answers to these questions, you need to do your homework. Speak to people who are already in this business, read trade papers or publications about the business, or contact government offices and professional or trade associations. You get help with some of this in Chapter 2.

The broader economy, the industry, and the specific market

Your personal life and practical resources may be in just the right shape for you to start your own business, but the business world will chew up and spit out a navel-gazer. You also need to look at the economy generally and at the market for your proposed product or service in particular.

If the economy is tanking, the time probably isn't right to launch a luxury business . . . but the time may be exactly right to start a business that will appeal to penny-pinchers. If the market for your product is jammed with competitors or if demand has started to dry up, you're headed for trouble if you stay on course. But if the market is just about to expand in a big way, you may have hit on a surefire success.

If and When to Give Up Your Day Job

Should you start a business and keep your day job (if you've got one)?

Conventional wisdom says that you shouldn't give up your day job until absolutely necessary (that's the point when you have to devote the time to your business or give it up) or until you don't need a day job (that's the point when you're making a living from your business). Conventional wisdom also urges entrepreneurs not to go it alone until they've saved up about six months' salary. That's a good joke. It would take most of us years to save six months' salary, unless we were offered a fantastic buyout package.

Even if you're dying to tell your current employer "I quit," think about the following questions:

- **Do you need the money from employment?** Even if your business turns out to be a success, you may not have much, or even any, income when you first start your business.

- **Do you want to keep your employment contacts?** The business you're starting might be something your employer or fellow employees can assist or patronize.

- **Do you have the time to hold down a job and start a business (and still have time to eat and sleep)?**

- **Would starting your own business and keeping your day job be problematic because of the following:**

  - Your employer's requirement (in your employment contract) that you not carry on any kind of a competing business while you're an employee?

  - Your employer's requirement (in your employment contract) that you put your full effort toward your employment work?

  - Suspicious superiors and coworkers who would assume you were goofing off by focusing on your own business instead of doing what you were paid to do?

- **Do you want to be able to fall back on your day job if your business venture doesn't work out?** Keep in mind that if you quit to start a business, you might not get hired back.

2

Seeking Out Helpful Business Information

How do you find the information you need to start your business? This chapter tells you how to collect data about the following areas:

- Starting and carrying on a business
- Acquiring general business skills
- Acquiring skills for your chosen business field

Basic Business Information

The amount of information about business can appear to be infinite. How do you home in on the information that's useful to you?

The first step is to get general information about starting and carrying on a business. Find a fairly comprehensive and self-contained start-to-finish source, such as a book — hey, this book is a great choice! — or a business resource centre, or a website. You've already got the book, so the following sections list suggestions for resource centres and websites. Start with the superstars, such as the Government of Canada's business resource portal. But don't forget to explore provincial and private sector resources.

The Government of Canada: Core resources for entrepreneurs

The Government of Canada maintains an online portal, referred to as Canada Business (www.canada business.ca), that provides access to both government and general business information, relevant to both start-up entrepreneurs and established, small to medium-size businesses in any field. This section shows you what you can expect to find there.

A look at the services offered

The Canada Business website provides information on government services, programs, and regulations pertaining to business. It has an extensive and up-to-date reference collection of general business information from government and nongovernment sources — topics include starting a business, writing a business plan, finding financing, marketing, exporting, and being an employer. Service centres located across Canada have information officers to help you navigate your way through everything they offer.

In addition, you can get products, services, publications, and referrals to experts. Here are some examples of the products and services the service centres provide:

- **Info guides:** These free guides on different topics provide brief overviews of services and programs.

- **How-to guides:** These guides provide information about the potential licence, permit, and registration requirements for specific types of businesses.

- **Fact sheets:** These fact sheets contain information about starting and running a business and are available online.

- **BizPaL online business permits and licences service:** This online service provides information about business permits and licence requirements from all levels of government.

- **Specialized Research Service:** This limited business research service is free and provides access to information on topics such as business associations, Canadian demographics, company data, consumer spending, and sample business plans.

Some of the service centres also offer low-cost seminars and workshops on a variety of business topics.

Access to the resources you need

 You can obtain resources in three ways:

- **Website:** The government's website (www.canada business.ca) contains information about business-related programs and services of federal and provincial agencies. The site allows you to input your province, industry, and/or demographic group and receive information tailored to the location and nature of your business; it also provides links to the individual websites maintained by some provinces.

  Some of the provincial sites also provide information about and let you register for business workshops and seminars, as well as links to other useful websites.

- **Email:** Send questions by email from the main website under Contact Us.

- **In person:** At the offices of your provincial/territorial service centre, you can use the resource materials on your own or with the help of a business information officer. These provincial service centres also have arrangements with existing business service organizations in communities across Canada to provide relevant information. Contact your Canada Business network service centre for the location nearest you. You can find information for your region at `http://canada business.ca/about/contact`.

Provincial and territorial government websites

Each provincial and territorial government maintains a website. Some of these sites contain good general business information that you can use to get started.

For example, the Nova Scotia site contains a "Business, nonprofit and self-employed" page with links to publications on planning, starting, and operating a business in Nova Scotia. The Manitoba site contains a list of business resources with links to information about starting, financing, and operating a business. The Ontario site is particularly helpful; its "Business and economy" page contains links to many useful sources.

 Here are the websites:

- **Alberta:** `www.gov.ab.ca`
- **British Columbia:** `www.gov.bc.ca`
- **Manitoba:** `www.gov.mb.ca`
- **New Brunswick:** `www.gov.nb.ca`
- **Newfoundland and Labrador:** `www.gov.nl.ca`

- **Northwest Territories:** www.gov.nt.ca
- **Nova Scotia:** www.gov.ns.ca
- **Nunavut:** www.gov.nu.ca
- **Ontario:** www.gov.on.ca
- **Prince Edward Island:** www.gov.pe.ca
- **Quebec:** www.quebec.ca
- **Saskatchewan:** www.gov.sk.ca
- **Yukon:** www.gov.yk.ca

Bank and trust company websites

The major banks' and trust companies' websites have information about the products and services they provide to small businesses. Some have information about general business topics, as well. For example, the Bank of Montreal business site (www.bmo.com/main/business) contains links to a number of small business resources such as podcasts, planning guides, articles, tips, Internet resources, and business FAQs.

Other bank websites include the Royal Bank of Canada (www.rbc.com), TD Canada Trust (www.td.com/ca/en/personal-banking), CIBC (www.cibc.com), HSBC (www.hsbc.com), and Scotiabank (www.scotiabank.com).

Small business or entrepreneurship centres

 A number of small business or entrepreneurship centres provide support and training to start-up and small businesses, for example:

- **Centennial College Centre of Entrepreneurship:** This Toronto-based centre provides entrepreneurial training, business plan development, analysis of proposed acquisitions, as-needed business advice and consulting, and international business training. It also offers a New Business Start-up Program, designed to provide entrepreneurs with the basic principles and practices of business, along with the skills to market, operate, and control a business. Visit `www.centennialcollege.ca/pdf/new-website/coe/be-your-own-boss.pdf` to find out more.

- **Centre for Entrepreneurship Education & Development (CEED):** This Nova Scotia not-for-profit society is devoted to helping people discover and use entrepreneurship as a vehicle to become self-reliant. Its services include technical assistance, entrepreneurship consulting, and entrepreneurship courses. CEED's website (`www.ceed.ca`) has more information.

- **Ontario Small Business Enterprise Centres:** These Ontario government centres are located throughout the province and provide entrepreneurs with support to start and grow their businesses. They offer a wide variety of support resources, including consultations with qualified business consultants, workshops and seminars, and mentoring and networking opportunities. Visit `www.ontario.ca/page/small-business-enterprise-centre-and-community-based-provider-locations` for more information.

- **The Stu Clark Centre for Entrepreneurship:** The University of Manitoba's Asper School of Business (`www.umanitoba.ca/asper`) operates this centre. It aims to encourage the development of new businesses and entrepreneurial thinking among Canadians. The centre supports a variety of programs aimed at youth, as well as undergraduate students and adults. The specific web page is `www.umanitoba.ca/faculties/management/academic_depts_centres/centres_institutes/entrepreneurship/index.html`.

Business incubators

A *business incubator* is a business mentoring facility that nurtures small and medium-size businesses during the start-up period. Business incubators provide management assistance, education, technical and business support services, and financial advice. They may also provide flexible rental space and flexible leases.

 More than 1,300 business incubators exist in North America, with about 170 located throughout Canada. Most Canadian business incubators are nonprofit and sponsored by government, economic development organizations, and academic institutions. Some examples of business incubators are

- **CDEM Business Incubator:** Run by the Economic Development Council for Manitoba Bilingual Municipalities and located in St. Boniface, Manitoba. Visit www.cdem.com/en for more information.

- **The Genesis Centre:** Located at the Memorial University of Newfoundland in St. John's. Their website is www.genesiscentre.ca.

- **Northern Alberta Business Incubator:** Created by and located in the city of St. Albert, Alberta. Their website is http://nabi.ca.

- **Toronto Business Development Centre (TBDC):** Started by the City of Toronto, TBDC's Business Incubation Program supports the growth of new businesses by providing useful resources, including business advisory support, dedicated office space, and participation in a robust community of successful entrepreneurs from around the world. Their website is www.tbdc.com.

The business incubator process usually has three stages:

- **Pre-incubation:** Applicants are screened for ability and compatibility with the business incubator's goals and may be referred for business skills training.

- **Incubation:** The business becomes a tenant of the business incubator and has access to the incubator's services for about three years.

- **Graduation:** The business moves into the community.

 Incubators are also known as *accelerators*. The slight nuance lies in the stage of start-ups they accept. Incubators are a resource for the "childhood" of a start-up, whereas accelerators can guide small business entrepreneurs from "adolescence" to "adulthood."

Information Geared to Your Specific Business

After you find out about starting and carrying on a business in general, you can find out more about your field of business in particular. For example, you might want to know these facts:

- What skills you need for this business
- What government regulations apply to this business
- How much it will cost to run this kind of business

- What the demand is for the goods or services you'll be supplying

- Who the likely customers are for the goods and services you'll provide

- What the competition is like for this type of business

- What supplies and equipment you require for this type of business

You need a good gateway into the sector you're interested in. Here are some recommendations.

Innovation, Science, and Economic Development Canada

The Innovation, Science, and Economic Development Canada website (www.ic.gc.ca) is particularly useful at the preliminary stage of starting a business because, in addition to general business information, it contains information on a wide variety of businesses, organized by sector. Each type of business has its own page, with additional pages on a number of subtopics. The subtopics vary for each business category but cover areas such as the following:

- **Company directories:** Links to lists of Canadian companies carrying on business in the field

- **Contacts:** Links to major trade associations in the field

- **Electronic business:** Links to a variety of information about e-business and e-commerce
- **Events:** Links to major trade shows in a particular business field
- **Grants:** Links to information about ways to fund your business with government assistance
- **Industry news:** Links to Canadian and American trade periodicals
- **Regulations and standards:** Links to relevant government regulations and standards organizations
- **Statistics, analysis, and industry profiles:** Links to North American Industry Classification definitions and to selected Canadian statistics on topics such as the Canadian market, imports, and exports
- **Trade and exporting:** Links to relevant international trade agreements and export information

Trade and professional associations

Trade and professional associations are another great source of information about particular fields of business. Thousands of associations exist in North America, many of them based in the United States. Whatever your field of business, a related association probably exists. A good association will give you access to industry-specific information.

Most associations maintain a website, setting out the services the association provides and membership information. Simon Fraser University has a web page with a repository of trade and professional associations that can be found at `www.lib.sfu.ca/help/research-assistance/subject/business/associations`. More general resources can be accessed at `www.cpmdq.com/htm/org.canada2.htm` and `www.canadiancareers.com/sector.html`.

The Internet is the best way to track down the trade or professional associations in your field. In your favorite search engine, type in the name of the specific field you're interested in plus the word *association* — for example, *giftware association.* You can also get information about associations on the Industry Canada website (`www.ic.gc.ca`).

Trade and professional journals

Many trade and professional associations publish journals or newsletters with current information about the field. They also contain ads for equipment and supplies that the business uses, and some list business opportunities (businesses for sale, partners wanted, premises for lease, equipment for sale, and so on).

You may be able to get information about trade and professional journals on the Innovation, Science, and Economic Development Canada website (`www.ic.gc.ca`).

Workshops and seminars

Many trade and professional associations hold seminars and workshops on topics of specific interest to members. Some offer courses leading to a designation or certification in the field.

Trade shows

Most trade associations hold an industry-wide trade show at least once a year. Trade shows are good places to make contacts in the industry and learn about the latest trends in the field.

Essential Business Skills

After you research your chosen business field, you may realize that you need some training before you can start your business. You may need skills specific to your chosen business field (such as how to frame a picture if you're going into the framing business, or how to mediate if you're going into family counselling), or you may want to pick up some general business skills and knowledge such as simple bookkeeping, basic computer skills, or how to prepare a business plan.

When people think of education, they usually think of universities, community colleges, career colleges, vocational schools, and boards of education. But in fact, many different places offer business education and skills training. You may be able to pick up the skills you need from a trade association, a partnering Canada Business network service centre, or the little place in your local mall that teaches keyboarding. In fact, you may want to avoid many of the educational institutions, because they often offer certificate or diploma programs more suited to people looking for a job, rather than individual courses focused on the specific skills an entrepreneur needs.

Where you go to get your training will depend on the kind of skill you're trying to acquire.

Skills for your particular business

You may be able to pick up the special skills required for your particular business in a day, a weekend, or a week. Or you may need a certificate or diploma in the field that will take months or years to get.

You may be able to find out not only what skills you need, but also where to get them, from Innovation, Science, and Economic Development Canada (www.ic.gc.ca) or from the relevant trade or professional association. Or you can use a search engine by typing in the name of the specific field you're interested in and the word *education* or *training*.

If you're not required to have a degree, diploma, or certificate offered by a university or community college, you may want to consider programs offered by privately run career colleges or vocational schools. These programs tend to be shorter than university and community college programs, but be warned: These courses are usually more expensive — sometimes much more expensive.

The trade or professional association in your field may offer short workshops or seminars on individual topics of interest to you, as well as complete training programs designed specifically for your field.

General business skills

To acquire in-depth business skills, you can enroll in degree, diploma, or certificate programs offered by colleges and universities. These programs run over the course of a year, or from two to three years. You probably won't be able to take one course of interest to you without taking another course as a prerequisite or without signing on for the entire program.

If you want to acquire some business skills as quickly as possible, look for continuing education courses offered by your local university or community college. For example, the University of Toronto (http://learn.utoronto.ca) and most other Canadian postsecondary institutions offer courses (usually with classes held once a week for about three months) in a wide variety of business-related areas, including accounting fundamentals, business law, business management, business strategy, social media strategy, and taxation for Canadian business. The University of Calgary (`http://conted.ucalgary.ca`) has seminars on numerous topics, including time management, accounting for nonfinancial managers, building great customer relationships, business writing basics, and creative negotiating.

Your local board of education may offer courses in business skills as part of its continuing education programs, and you should have no problem enrolling in individual courses rather than in programs. Classes will probably be scheduled once a week over several months.

You may also be able to find weekend workshops or evening seminars offered by your trade or professional association, or through your provincial Canada Business network service centre.

3

Choosing a Product
or Service

Your business will be in big trouble if you offer a product or service that not a soul wants or that your chosen customer group is not interested in. This chapter helps you avoid those problems and give you hints on how to develop a product or service tailored for your target customers or clients.

How to Develop a Product or Service with a Market in Mind

To start a business, you need a product or service to sell. And it needs to be something that customers or clients want to buy.

Developing a product or service requires quite a chunk of your time and energy. You'll need to take on some tasks that may seem kind of challenging, such as researching potential customers and existing competition.

Eureka!

To start at the beginning, where do ideas for products or services come from in the first place? Very innocent entrepreneurs believe that the stork brings ideas, or that ideas are found in the garden under the fallen leaves of maple trees. But entrepreneurs who've been introduced to the facts of life know that ideas really come from the following sources:

- **Potential customers:** If you're not actually in business yet, you don't have customers, but you're probably already in contact with people who would be glad to be your customers if only you'd provide a product or service they need. Keep your ears open in your current job — maybe your employer or your employer's competitors or your employer's customers or suppliers are making wistful comments about not being able to find Product X, or Person Y to perform Service Z.

- **Trade shows, trade journals — even the daily newspaper or a TV program:** A great idea may already be out there. It just needs you to develop it.

- **Your fertile imagination:** You may have had a real *eureka!* moment, when you thought up a solution to a problem or you created an invention that people have been desperately hoping for — or that they don't even know they need yet.

Ask yourself some sobering questions

After the *eureka!* moment has passed and your heart rate has returned to normal, you need to rationally evaluate the idea. Love at first sight can cost you a lot in business (just like in real life), so you have to make sure that this is the idea for you to get hitched up with. This section looks at deciding whether

- This is the right idea for you and your business personality.
- A market exists for the product or service you envision.
- You can compete successfully.
- The idea is financially viable.

If your idea is new and innovative, you may be able to get assistance with the evaluation — for example, from the Canadian Innovation Centre (CIC) (www. innovationcentre.ca) in Waterloo, Ontario, an organization that grew out of the invention commercialization activities of the University of Waterloo. The CIC's website has information for inventors, as well as links to other useful organizations such as the U.S. National Inventor Fraud Center (www. inventor-fraud.com), which offers advice on how to steer away from invention marketing companies that are set up only to scam inventors.

 Don't get mixed up with a company that combines high-pressure sales tactics with a low success rate.

Is this idea right for you?

Or is this a good idea at all, when you get right down to it? For example, is it legal? (And if it's legal now, will it become illegal after it takes off? Remember radar detectors for the travelling public?) Is it hands-off? The reverse is also true. Chapter 4 discusses the whole area of cannabusiness, a business sphere that was generally illegal just a while ago, but is now legal. The idea may already be patented and the patent owner doesn't want to license to you.

Are you legal? Some products and services can be provided only by a licensed individual or business. Is the product or service safe — or will you cause harm to someone and end up getting sued? And if everything's legal, hands-on, and safe, do you have the reputation or expertise needed to develop the idea into a business and reel in customers or clients?

Does anyone want the product or service?

Your idea may seem wonderful to you, but you're going to need a slightly larger market than yourself to prosper. So, you have to do some *customer research* — identify a target market for the product or service and estimate the size of the market. Here's a brief guide to doing customer research.

First, think generally about who your customers or clients might be (keep in mind that you can be wrong about this, though). For example, are they

- **Other businesses?** A whole bunch of them or just one or two? Are the businesses service providers or retailers or manufacturers?

- **Individuals?** Do the individuals live in a particular neighbourhood or geographic area, or do they live all over the country or around the world? Are they men only? Women only? The young? Older people? The well-to-do, or just anyone with a buck to spend?

After you've identified a starting point, you can proceed with your customer research to find out if anybody would want your product or service. Different research methods exist, so try a combination of them. From the least expensive to most expensive, here they are:

- **Review of publicly available information:** This includes websites (including blogs), TV programs, newspapers, trade journals, newsletters, and market analysis materials from the business reference section of a public or university library.

- **Direct observation of potential customers or clients:** You can use your own personal knowledge of a business you're in or you've followed, you can visit stores and trade shows, or you can attend presentations and conferences.

- **Interviews with experts in the field or with potential customers or clients:** This isn't as hard to do as you think. If you start with people you know and ask for names of other people who wouldn't mind talking to you, if you just ask for an opinion or advice and don't try to sell anything, and if you keep the interview polite and brief, you will very likely meet people who will agree to give you 20 minutes or half an hour of their time. It's really amazing how many people are open and amenable to sharing their thoughts and insights, especially if you compliment them by referring to them as experts or thought leaders in their field.

 Try to meet face-to-face if you can — the interviewee will remember you better if it later turns out that she needs the product or service you want to provide.

- **Focus groups:** See if you can lure groups of potential customers or clients together to talk about the product or service. The lure should be something significant, like a free meal or a chance to win a prize. Unless you

can find friends and acquaintances who'll participate
in a focus group, you may be better off hiring a market
analysis firm to run focus groups than trying to corner
strangers on your own.

- **Surveys and questionnaires:** These are short written,
telephone or online questionnaires distributed or con-
ducted on a large scale. You'll have to come up with
the right questions to ask, and pay for printing and
distribution of written materials, find your nerve to
make calls or hire trained interviewers to phone
people at dinnertime, and then you'll have to analyze
the results . . . if anyone answers the questions (a lot of
paper surveys will be considered garbage and thrown
out, and a lot of people won't answer telephone
interviewers).

Doing door-to-door surveys in a neighbourhood, or
approaching people on the street in a business or
shopping area, will probably earn you a lot of suspi-
cion and brush-offs. As with focus groups, you may
prefer to have a professional market analysis firm
handle a survey. (Surveys and questionnaires are easier to handle yourself if you already have an established customer base.)

At the conclusion of your market research, ideally you
should have an idea about whether the product or service is
attractive to some target group(s), and you should also be able

to estimate roughly the size of your market. Your market is the number of customers you'll win times the number of sales per customer.

Who's the competition?

And what are they up to? This information is known as *competitive intelligence.* Your competitors may already have claimed all the customers or clients you identified by doing your market research. Or they may not. You can find out by assessing your potential market share.

To start with the question just asked ("Who's the competition?"), your competition is made up of the following:

- **Direct competitors:** Those who offer exactly the same product or service
- **Indirect competitors:** Those who offer an alternative product that more or less meets the same need as your product
- **Who-was-that-masked-man? competitors:** Those who offer something completely different that potential customers will spend their money on instead of on your product or a similar product, much to your regret and amazement
- **Inertia:** The tendency of customers and clients to do nothing at all when brought face-to-face with your wonderful product or service

As an example, if you want to offer a service tutoring children in math or reading, your direct competition is other private tutoring services, your indirect competition is the public and private schools in the area (they may be doing a fine job of teaching, in which case your services won't be required); your who-was-that-masked-man? competition is social media and video games; and inertia is parents letting their kids sink or swim through school on their own.

 Look carefully at your direct and indirect competitors and see if you can find out whether

- They've cornered the market and are doing such a good job at such a good price that you don't have much hope of taking market share away from them. Or whether you should be able to relieve them of market share because you can offer better value — for example, a lower price, a higher-quality product or service, a more convenient location, greater expertise, friendlier service, and so on. Sometimes the first competitor into the market may just have collected and educated your potential clients for you!

- Their business is profitable — are they growing or shrinking?

- They're big enough and mean enough to run you out of town if you show your face on the street (have you noticed how small airlines regularly get eaten?).

How much money can you put behind this idea?

You likely can't get your idea off the ground for free. So, the last sober second thought involves figuring out

- **Approximately how much it will cost to launch your business:** This involves adding up your start-up costs plus bridge financing for your operating expenses until your business is generating income.

- **Approximately how much money is available to you for a business start-up:** The cash you have on hand or can raise through family contributions may be enough to get your particular business up and running; or you may need a bank loan for a larger amount; or you may need a significant investment from an angel investor or venture capital firm. (See Chapter 5 for sources of start-up money.)

   How much you'll be able to raise (especially from outsiders) is linked to the likely return on investment (ROI) for your idea. So, just because it will take $1 million to build a plant to produce your product doesn't mean you should scrap the idea. It can be full steam ahead if an investor believes that your business can generate profits of $2 million annually after a couple of years or that the business might be worth $50 million in five years.

Tinker with your idea

After you've had all these second thoughts, you have to decide whether to forget your idea altogether or rework it in light of what you've discovered about your target market and your competition. If you decide to keep going with your idea, you may be thinking about how you can do the following:

- Redesign or add value to the product or service so that it appeals more to your target market
- Provide the product or service more efficiently than the competition or at a price that potential customers or clients will find more attractive
- Redesign or reposition your product or service so that it doesn't meet a powerful competitor head-on
- Redesign or present the product or service so that it appeals to a potential investor

After you've tinkered, you may need to re-evaluate.

The Best Route to Your Target Market

Okay, so you think you've got a product or service that can go the distance. Now you have to figure out how to get it from you to the person who will actually use it — so you have to decide on one or more distribution channels. You have two basic choices:

- **Distribute directly.** The product or service goes from your business to your buyer (most services and products take this route).
- **Distribute indirectly.** The product or service goes from your business to another business to the buyer. Although your target market is the buyer, your customer is the "middleman" business.

From your business directly to your customer

If you choose direct distribution, you can deal with customers or clients in two ways:

- **Face-to-face:** In your retail store or office.
- **Facelessly:** Through an order system that uses a website, email, mail, phone, or even fax. If you choose this option, note that you'll need a place to keep your inventory, such as a room in a warehouse, and you'll need a delivery system, such as mail or a courier. (Certain kinds of services provided this way — such as essays or advice for the lovelorn — may be deliverable electronically.)

From your business to another business to your target customer

If your customer is a middleman, you'll probably need fewer customers to make a go of your business. However, a middleman may be more demanding about low prices, so your profit margin may be lower.

Middlemen include

- **Retailers**
- **Wholesalers or distributors:** They, in turn, sell to retailers, and sometimes to the general public.
- **Re-packagers:** They also sell to retailers after — you guessed it — repackaging the products they buy from you.

You may be able to or may want to sell directly to the middleman yourself, or you may want to employ a manufacturer's agent or representative to do the selling for you (on commission). First, you'll have to choose an agent who sells to the kind of middleman you want in the regions you want. Then you'll have to persuade the agent to carry your line and talk it up to customers.

How to Price Your Product or Service

You can make a profit in different ways — for example, by combining a small profit on each item or service provided with high sales volume, or by combining a low sales volume with a big profit on each transaction. (Best, of course, is high profit on each unit and high sales volume, but not many businesses are that lucky.) But if you underprice, you'll lose money on every sale even if you sell a gazillion units; if you overprice, no one will buy at all. How do you figure this whole thing out? This section talks about how to settle on the right price to charge.

Decide on the minimum price you can charge

Minimum price is not all that difficult to figure out. As a rule, you don't want to charge less for your product or service than it costs to produce. (An exception to the rule is offering the product or service as a loss leader, to lure customers in — but you can't keep that up for long, and certainly not on an important part of your line.) The formula that tells you, as the owner of a start-up business, your cost to produce (your *break-even cost*) is the following:

Total Direct and Indirect Costs over a Given Period ÷
Total Number of Products or Services That It Would Be
Reasonable for You to Provide over the Given Period =
Your Break-Even Cost for That Period

Your break-even cost for the period is the amount you need
to charge for each unit of your product or service to pay your
direct and indirect costs (see the next section).

Direct costs, also known as variable costs, include

- Materials required to manufacture the product, and cost
  of shipping the materials to your site
- Lease payments for factory space or storage space
- Energy (or other utility) costs of production (for example, electricity and water)
- Wages paid to subcontractors or employees to produce
  the product or service
- Cost of delivering the product or service to your
  customer

Indirect costs, also known as fixed costs or overhead,
include administrative expenses such as the following:

- Wages for office staff
- Electricity, telephone, and other office utilities
- Office supplies
- Advertising expenses
- Rent on your office space

If your business involves supplying a service rather than manufacturing a product, you'll probably have higher indirect costs than direct costs.

Decide on the maximum price you can charge

Now over to the other end of the price scale. Here, the ceiling for your price is the value of your product or service to the customer or client. Value is what the customer perceives that he or she is getting in exchange for the cost of the product, and includes things such as quality and reliability of the product or service, image or prestige associated with the product or service, uniqueness of the product or service, backup from your business such as support and guarantees, convenience of dealing with your business (such things as good location or inexpensive delivery or the helpfulness of your staff), and incentives such as *rebates* (money back following a purchase), *discounts* (money off the purchase price), and other freebies.

If customers believe that your price (their cost) is greater than the value of your product or service (the benefit to them), customers won't buy from you.

Table 3-1 is a sample break-even chart that you can use to calculate the sales volume at which you'll break even.

Direct or variable cost per month of producing total number of units you think it would be reasonable to produce and sell in a month (let's say 1,000, at $10 per unit)	$10,000
PLUS	
Indirect or fixed cost per month of producing the units	$5,000
EQUALS	
Total cost per month of producing the units	$15,000
DIVIDED BY	
Number of units of product or service produced and sold per month	1,000
EQUALS	
Break-even cost, or the minimum *price* you need to charge per unit	$15

Table 3-1: *A Sample Break-Even Chart*

You can fiddle with the figures in the different boxes, increasing or decreasing the numbers to see how your break-even cost is affected by changes. This is referred to as a *sensitivity analysis,* and it's a great tool for making scenario-based decisions. For example, if your direct cost is $12,000 instead of $10,000, your minimum price becomes $17. Or if the number of units produced and sold is 800 instead of 1,000, your minimum price becomes $18.75 instead of $15.

 A Microsoft Excel spreadsheet is a great tool to use for these types of arithmetic gymnastics.

Set your price

Setting a price comes down to supply and demand. If a product is essential or useful and it's hard to find, the price can be higher and the product will still sell (until people run out of money). If a product is not a must-have or is readily available, the price has to be lower if you want to sell. Higher or lower than what? The competition's price.

So, see what your competition is charging. When you know that, then you can implement one of the following three strategies:

- **Charge more than the competition.** This will work only if your product is seen as more valuable than the competition's. You can increase the value of the same product or service offered by the competition by, for example, creating a higher-end image for your business or trading on your reputation as an expert.

- **Charge the same as the competition.** But you still need to increase the value of your product over the competition's to drive actual sales. You can do this, for example, by offering a more convenient location to your target customers.

- **Charge less than the competition.** Just be careful not to undercut your own cost of production, and keep in mind that you'll acquire a "reputation." Whether it's true or not, customers and clients will tend to associate lower prices with lower value. Only in rare cases will people think they've made a marvellous discovery of a business that carries exactly the same product as the competition, but at a lower price. It's also a good idea to keep prices fluid. Flexibility never hurts.

Whether You Should Consider a Franchise

A *franchise* isn't exactly an off-the-shelf business. It's more like a prepackaged business — you add water and stir. The *franchisor* (the company that created and developed the original business) owns the business name, trademarks, and practices and procedures; the *franchisee* (the "buyer" of the franchise, who is essentially granted the rights to the franchise) gets a licence to use them. The franchisee pays an upfront franchise fee and then also makes continuing payments (royalties) based on the franchise's earnings. The franchisee sets up his or her own business, but sets it up as if it were part of a chain with one name and with standardized products, design, service, and operations.

The advantages of a franchise

Being granted the rights to an established franchise provides the benefits of belonging to a large organization, while still being your own boss, including

- A business concept that has been thought out, and a product or service that has been researched and developed
- A recognized business name, centralized advertising, and sophisticated marketing
- Assistance, training, and support in management and production
- Economies of scale in buying supplies and services, because purchasing is centralized
- Assistance in choosing a business location (reputable franchises check out the strength of the local market before selling a new franchise in an area)

The disadvantages of a franchise

Buying a franchise can sometimes lead to trouble for the franchisee because

- Franchises like Harvey's are standardized operations, and standardization can be stifling to a business owner who has his or her own ideas.

- Successful franchises like McDonald's are very expensive — and new franchises are a gamble because costs may be higher than expected and/or profits lower than expected.

- Franchise agreements are always drafted by the franchisor and they favour the franchisor over the franchisee.

- The franchisor may promise training and support, but they may not be as good or thorough as promised.

- Franchisees may be charged more than the going market rate for supplies if they have to be purchased through the franchisor or specified suppliers.

- Franchisees are often required to pay substantial amounts for advertising, and they may not see that they're getting anything in return.

- Sometimes the franchisor leases premises for a franchise location and subleases them to the franchisee. Then the franchisor can use its rights as a landlord to lock the franchisee out of the premises without notice if the franchisee doesn't make all the payments required under the franchise agreement.

- If the franchisor opens too many coffee shops in one area, for example, or starts distributing products through eBay or Shopify, it can drastically reduce the profits of franchisees.

- Franchisees often don't have special legislation to protect them against franchisors, because only about half of
the provinces to date have passed franchise statutes.

How to find a franchise

Franchises are available in just about any business area, from
accounting and tax services to pet care to lawn services to
senior care services. So the first step in finding a franchise is to
decide on the kind of business you want to be in.

After you decide on the kind of business you want to be in,
find out whether any franchises exist in that kind of business,
and if so, whether any franchises are being offered in the location you're interested in.

 You can look for franchises that are available in
Canada in a number of ways:

- **Read franchise magazines.** A number of magazines
are geared to people interested in buying a franchise,
such as *Canadian Business Franchise Magazine* (www.
franchiseinfo.ca) and *Franchise Canada* (http://
franchisecanada.cfa.ca), the official publication
of the Canadian Franchise Association (CFA). These
magazines and resources contain general information
and advice about franchising and contain ads for
franchises for sale.

- **Check a franchise directory.** The Franchise Canada Directory (www.cfa.ca/franchisecanada/franchisecanada-directory), published by the Canadian Franchise Association, lists available franchises.

- **Search the Internet.** Many websites contain information about franchises for sale. The Canadian Franchise Association's website (www.cfa.ca) contains a "Look for a Franchise" feature that allows you to browse franchises either by name or by category. Only CFA members in good standing are listed. You can also check BeTheBoss.ca (www.betheboss.ca) or FranchiseSolutions.com (www.franchisesolutions.com).

- **Visit franchise shows.** A number of franchise shows are held across Canada throughout the year, such as the Franchise Expo (www.franchiseshowinfo.com) and the Franchise Show (www.cfa.ca/events/franchise-canada-show), which is organized by the Canadian Franchise Association.

- **Use a franchise advisor.** Some accounting firms, such as BDO Dunwoody or Grant Thornton, provide help in finding and evaluating potential franchises. You can also find business brokers who deal in the resale of existing franchises.

4

Considering a Cannabusiness

If a Bay Street businessperson picks up the dictionary, he or she will find that the term *cannabusiness* means "the commercial activity of selling cannabis or cannabis-based products." If a hipster goes to the Urban Dictionary, he or she will see that *cannabusiness* means "the fine art of selling weed." Either definition is fine.

Cannabusiness is becoming a real powerhouse force in the Canadian economy. A discussion about its somewhat long history in Canada is beyond the scope of this book, but it's worth noting that this sector truly awakened in 2018 when use of recreational cannabis became legal. The Cannabis Act is the law that legalized recreational cannabis use in Canada, in tandem with its companion legislation Bill C-46, An Act to Amend the Criminal Code. When this act was passed, Canadians witnessed the birth of a whole new business sector.

Ever since, and a bit before, Canada's leadership in the marijuana sector has made the world stand up and take notice. There is an endless stream of news — good and bad — about the issues surrounding this sector. As everyone knows, where there is change, there is also opportunity, and Canadian small business entrepreneurs and those who want to be "cannapreneurs" are stepping up to the plate to consider taking a swing at the opportunity. If you're one of those folks, this chapter is for you.

How to Determine If You Have What It Takes

Chapter 1 outlines the upsides and downsides of small business ownership. If cannabusiness is the industry sector you're interested in, the principles discussed in that chapter don't change. However, because this is a brand-new frontier for Canadians, both the upsides and the downsides may be more pronounced than they are for existing and longstanding industries in Canada. Uncertainty fuels the volatility and velocity of change, as well as how pronounced the impacts of that change may be. So, if you're interested in getting into the cannabusiness sector, you need to be able to tolerate a little volatility, and go with the flow, man.

If you've never experienced the culture of cannabis, you may be at a disadvantage. To catch up, check out the later section "A plant by any other name: The lingo" to at least *pretend* you regularly talk the talk. If you want to do business in the legitimate marijuana ecosystem, you need to speak two languages — one related to the traditional cannabis subculture, and the other that of the real business world. With a mix of grow-culture speak and MBA-style business savvy, you'll do well in the legitimate cannabis ecosystem.

Your success is also most likely to crystallize if you and your employees are able to adapt to changes in the cannabis industry, and keep up with growing amounts of legislation at both the federal and provincial/territorial levels. It also helps if you have a creative streak in order to adapt your existing skill set, background, and experience into a brand-new small cannabusiness context. Do you have these and other similar traits?

Another acid test (no drug pun intended) is to really ask yourself if you're "just sort of" interested in cannabis or if you're totally amped about it. If it's the former, success may be harder to find. That's because starting a business is hard enough in longstanding industries; it's even harder in the undiscovered country of cannabusiness. Participating in the cannabis industry requires that you're committed to the hard work and effort associated with understanding dozens of aspects of the sector.

A good approach to making sure you have the right stuff is to leverage what you're really good at. Wield your very best *soft skills* (such as interpersonal and relationship building skills), and leverage your tangible background and experience. Get other outside experts or your own employees to help you with the rest. For example, creative agencies can build your website, and graphic designers can help with your marketing materials.

Be one of the three musketeers and adopt an "all for one, one for all" philosophy. Collaborate when you must, join forces and resources, and work as a team to maximize your chances for greater market share.

Helpful Business Information

Chapter 2 shows you how to search for relevant information about business in general, as well as investigate your own field (in this case, cannabusiness). You also find out how you can build your skill set with online and other resources. If you haven't read that chapter yet, take a quick look — it's a logical reference point for this chapter.

If you want to start a cannabusiness, knowing the rules of the game is critical. The laws, rules, and regulatory framework for opening a cannabusiness are incredibly complex, growing, and fast-changing. The pace of legislative change, combined with the fact that this is an emerging industry and sector, make knowing the regulations, risks, and theory around cannabusiness imperative to your business success.

Industry information

A good place to start your quest for knowledge of cannabusiness is to understand the theoretical side of the legal marijuana business. This section covers the basics, as well as cannabusiness industry trends.

A plant by any other name: The lingo

You may have heard the terms *marijuana* and *cannabis* and wondered about the difference. Here's the deal: *Marijuana* refers to the plant scientifically known as *cannabis* — more specifically, to three recognized species that include *Cannabis sativa*, *Cannabis indica*, and *Cannabis ruderalis*.

The cannabis plant is a source of hundreds of compounds. Two in particular, called delta-9-tetrahydrocannabinol (THC) and cannabidiol, are the most widely tested elements for medicinal and recreational uses. *Hemp*, another term you hear lots about, is a variety of the *Cannabis sativa* plant species that is grown specifically for the industrial uses of its derived products.

So, next time you hear news stories about marijuana, you'll likely hear about these terms. You'll also realize that marijuana and cannabis refer to the same plant, so from here on, this chapter uses the terms *cannabis* and *marijuana* interchangeably.

Cannabis looks weird. The shredded flowers, buds, and leaves of a marijuana plant comes in a green, brown, or gray mix. It's smelly, too. Cannabis is presented in various ways and forms. Marijuana that is rolled up like a cigarette is called a *joint*, and if you roll it like a cigar, it's a *blunt*. Marijuana can also be smoked in a *pipe*. Some Canadians incorporate marijuana into cookies or other foods, or brew it as a flavoured tea. Canadians who smoke oils from the marijuana plant practice what is referred to as *dabbing*. Other slang names for marijuana include *pot, weed, grass, herb,* or *boom*.

What's happening with weed today

It's also interesting to note that smoking weed isn't the main trend. Actually, quite a few pot users are turning away from the smoking variety of marijuana. The smoke has a problem: People's lungs get coated and choked with tar under long-term use. More and more users are tending toward new ways to consume pot. These alternative ways to consume, not all legal yet, include vaporizing, eating cannabis-infused foods like crackers, drinking cannabis-infused lemonade, ingesting oils taken in capsules or added to food or drink, applying tinctures directly under the tongue, and using topical lotions and balms. Do you see the brand-new industries cropping up? The trend is your friend. Know the trends if you want to pursue cannabusiness success.

This is not a health book or chapter. But do know about what people, perhaps your customers, may experience. Cannabis can make you feel relaxed, silly, sleepy, and happy. It can also make you nervous and scared. Your senses of hearing, sight, and touch may be altered. Your judgement may also be significantly impaired.

Why you may want to invest in a cannabusiness

As with any new industry, there are good opportunities to be found for Canadian cannabusiness entrepreneurs willing to do their research, and who recognize the advantages and trends. One advantage is the fact that Canada has provided other countries with a legal and operational template for politicians and producers to mimic. In other words, the fact that Canada has first mover advantage in a politically friendly context makes the opportunity to invest in this industry undeniable. But, of course, the risks of doing so are still many.

It's also an advantage that medicinal pot is already entrenched in the Canadian healthcare industry, so it already has a small but important installed base market. What better endorsement is there than a hospital or doctor sanctioning its careful use? As all this slow but steady acceptance is happening, the investment community has swooped in for a piece of the action. The flow of capital is vital (and something you need to watch) in order for any emerging sector to grow and flourish.

The trend is your friend. Let's take a look at where we've been so far, with numbers, which always tell part of a story. Arcview Market Research, a prominent marijuana market research company, reported that legal pot sales way back in 2017 were $10 billion in North America. The company has since estimated that by the end of 2021, sales can reach $25 billion or more. That's a big enchilada of a number. At the time of this writing, there are more than 100 publicly listed companies in Canada supporting this ecosystem, with a market capitalization value of $35 billion.

Go to the Marijuana Index (www.marijuanaindex. com) to access indexes for the North American, American, and Canadian marijuana stock markets. Why stock markets? Because stock market indexes are excellent indicators of what investors think of the potential of a sector, industry, or individual company. It's a great proxy for the health of the weed sector as a whole. It's also a great site to visit for basic news information on the sector. Four hundred companies are listed.

The basic infrastructure — access to financial markets, the ability to produce marijuana, and lots of smart visionaries with sound business plans — is now in place, and the ecosystem is thriving. Now that cannabis is legal, other indicators of growth to watch for include new listings of large Canadian cannabis companies on major American exchanges like the New York Stock Exchange (NYSE) or Nasdaq. Tilray, Inc. (TLRY); Canopy Growth Corporation (CGC); Cronos Group, Inc. (CRON); and Aurora Cannabis (ACB) have all benefitted from listing with our friends south of the border. Many others are applying.

Also, watch for merger and acquisition activity for a barometer of industry health. Recently, Aurora Cannabis made a $3 billion all-stock offer to buy its rival and licensed producer MedReleaf to create an 800-pound gorilla in the cannabis sector. Together, the combined company is poised to produce more than 600,000 kilograms of cannabis annually, representing about 50 percent of expected Canadian demand in 2021.

What other countries do is critical as well. Look for developments in Italy, Sweden, and, of course, the United States to see if their markets will further open up domestic, as well as foreign, supply of medical and legal marijuana. And see how many American companies are seeking listings on Canadian exchanges. If banks like BMO and others support the industry, that's another great sign that the sector will continue to thrive. It will help point you to promising business ideas and areas.

Although American laws and Food and Drug Administration (FDA) regulations are still in a state of flux, you'd be wise to wonder if the United States represents the next big opportunity and super-catalyst. If so, then Canadian suppliers are uniquely poised to capitalize. That's because Canada is one of only two countries — the other is the Netherlands — that currently exports cannabis (if you have a license and the purpose is medical or scientific) to well over 20 countries. It also helps the future of this sector that the number of companies that have been authorized by Health Canada to produce medicinal marijuana across the country has been steadily increasing.

To get statistics and market forecast information, check out the Statistics Canada website at www. statcan.gc.ca and use the search tool with the term *cannabis* or *marijuana.* You can find lots of current and helpful information on this rapidly evolving industry sector.

Legal and regulatory information

Whether you use marijuana or simply want to start a business in this budding (no pun intended) industry, you can get into real legal or financial trouble. But that trouble only comes if you don't know and follow the rules, be they rules about growing, processing, retailing, or any other aspect such as licensing. A good starting point to avoiding trouble is knowing the specific rules and regulations in place about marijuana today.

Canada was a pioneer in the legalized use of marijuana for medical purposes as far back as two decades ago. Today, it's also legally permitted to purchase, grow, and possess limited, regulated, and tested amounts of cannabis in Canada. Way back in 2014, it was actually already legal for Canadian medical patients to possess medical marijuana from a licensed distributor, but only with a prescription provided by a still-practicing Canadian physician. Soon after, legislation evolved to allow patients possessing a prescription from a doctor to grow their own medical marijuana plant and use the bud. They can even designate a third-party grower to grow it for them. The Cannabis Act, together with provincial and territorial legislation, currently prescribe the number of cannabis plants that can be grown per household, as well as any other key restrictions.

Canada now possesses a draft but rigid legal framework to oversee the production, distribution, sale, and possession of cannabis across Canada. This framework has allowed for the legal, efficient, and effective production and cultivation of cannabis. The good news is that the new legislation is aimed at restricting access to cannabis by underaged Canadian youth, deterring and reducing crime around it, and protecting the users of the drug through strict safety requirements and quality control measures. Also, the legacy program for accessing cannabis for medical purposes will continue under the new act. As you can see, it's really important for cannapreneurs to understand the ever-changing legalities — and opportunities — surrounding the medical marijuana industry. It's crucial to be a good cannabis ecosystem citizen.

If you're like most news-watching Canadians, you've undoubtedly heard about occasional raids on pot dispensaries on Queen Street in Toronto, West Hastings Street in Vancouver, and elsewhere all across Canada. That's because, even under the new law, some dispensaries may be operating illegally. Canadians who buy medical marijuana from an unproven dispensary are also placing themselves at risk of possible exposure to pesticides, heavy toxic metals, and nasty pathogens. Starting a cannabusiness is complex.

Why following the rules is so important

Knowing the rules really well is the first step to making sure you don't break them. This is important because the penalties for breaking drug-, health-, and safety-related rules are much more severe than they are for breaking other laws of the land. These penalties include large fines and even jail time. To manage the legal and regulatory risks of noncompliance with the rules, you first have to identify and understand what those rules and, therefore, risks are. In addition, legal and regulatory risks are just one of many risks that cannabusinesses face. We deal with these risks throughout this chapter.

To start and run your cannabusiness, make sure that you and your employees possess a sound understanding of how the regulations work and how and where to get more information when necessary.

 When the rules become overwhelming, it is *strongly* recommended that you hire an experienced lawyer with cannabis-related expertise to help you along.

The cannabis industry is still in its infancy and many new regulations are still hot off the press. This makes networking with local institutions and industry associations important in order to get their guidance and insights. The next section shows you some starting points and approaches to help.

Government of Canada resources

To stay on top of the shifting sands of federal legislation, check out the Government of Canada's Cannabis in Canada website (www.canada.ca/cannabis) for key details that will expand your knowledge of the industry. These details include essential information about law, medicine, and educational resources pertinent to cannabis.

For example, the website advises you not to travel with cannabis across the border, and identifies the risks of impairment on the road and at work. For cannabusinesses, the key tab to check out on this website is What Industry Needs to Know; here, you can find out how the Canadian legal and regulatory framework may impact your cannabusiness.

There are federal rules and provincial and territorial rules. Whether your business will transact in only one province or in several provinces, you need to know what is legal in each province and territory across Canada.

After the Cannabis Act and its supporting regulations became law on October 17, 2018, Health Canada became the main government entity accepting applications from those who want to become cannabis licence holders and comply with the act.

At the time of this writing, Health Canada was in the process of making amendments to the cannabis regulations that would enable licensed processors to produce and sell three new classes of cannabis: edible cannabis, cannabis extracts, and cannabis topicals. The legal production and sale of edible cannabis, cannabis extracts, and cannabis topicals is expected to be permitted by October 17, 2019.

As indicated on the Cannabis in Canada website, cannabis licence holders may actually need not one but two licences: one from Health Canada and, possibly, one from the Canada Revenue Agency (CRA).

You're required to have a licence from Health Canada if you want to grow cannabis commercially for sale or produce cannabis products commercially. You also need a licence from Health Canada if you sell cannabis for medical purposes, conduct scientific tests on cannabis, and/or conduct research with cannabis.

On the Cannabis in Canada website, click the What Industry Needs to Know link, and then click Apply for or Amend a Licence. Check this website regularly for any changes to the requirements.

The federal government requires that cultivators, producers, and packagers of cannabis products obtain a special cannabis licence from the CRA. It doesn't stop there. After you obtain a license, you're also required to buy and apply cannabis excise stamps (explained at www.canada.ca/en/ revenue-agency/campaigns/cannabis-taxation) to your products (if you package cannabis products), calculate the duty on your sales, and file a return and send the excise duty to the CRA.

 Health Canada runs an online Cannabis Tracking and Licensing System. This system allows you to submit and view the status of applications. It also allows you to submit amendments to licences. You can access it at www.canada.ca/cannabis by clicking the What Industry Needs to Know link.

Your cannabusiness has to follow plain packaging and labelling standards in order to protect against accidental consumption, to ensure that products are not appealing to minors and youth, and to provide consumers with key information they need to make informed decisions prior to consuming canna-bis. Health Canada prescribes the rules around packaging; you can find out more at `www.canada.ca/en/health-canada/services/drugs-medication/cannabis/laws-regulations/regulations-support-cannabis-act.html`.

Cannabusiness owners, whether they're licensed or not, absolutely must comply with the Cannabis Act and its associ-ated and relevant regulations. This means that you're expected to know and understand the legislation and your obligations, cooperate with inspectors, and comply with orders and prohi-bitions from Health Canada. Health Canada's compliance and enforcement policy can be found at `www.canada.ca/en/health-canada`. Check it out to see what parts of the long arm of the law apply to your business idea or enterprise.

The rules are also very tight regarding what and how you can market. The prohibitions against cannabis marketing under the Cannabis Act apply to you if you promote canna-bis, cannabis accessories, and services related to cannabis. The vital details can be found at `www.canada.ca/en/health-canada/services/drugs-medication/cannabis/laws-regulations/promotion-prohibitions`. You can also just Google the term *prohibitions for cannabis marketing in Canada* to get not just the government's website but also arti-cles on the subject as well. The provinces and territories have something to say as well, and knowing these rules is critical.

Check them out at www.canada.ca/en/health-canada/
services/drugs-medication/cannabis/laws-
regulations/provinces-territories. For example,
Ontario made changes by capping the number of new retail
cannabis stores that can open annually in the province. This
is a significant new restriction.

Fees apply to you on the following classes of licences:

- Cultivation (standard, micro, or nursery)

- Processing (standard or micro)

- Sales for medical purposes

These fees are meant to recover costs for screening your
licence application, executing security screening, and review-
ing the substance of the applications to import or export cannabis for scientific or medical purposes. The fees also cover a
robust review of your licence application, the actual issuance
of your licences (if you're successful), inspections, and compliance and enforcement activities.

If you're involved in the cannabis industry in Canada,
you should know that the legalization of cannabis in
Canada has not changed Canada's border rules. It's
still illegal to take cannabis across Canada's international borders. The Canadian government's website
states the following: "If you try to travel internationally with any amount of cannabis in your possession,

you can be subject to serious criminal penalties both at home and abroad. You can also be denied entry at your destination country if you have previously used cannabis or any substance prohibited by local laws."

No cannabusiness may export or import cannabis for any purposes, other than for medical or scientific purposes, under the Cannabis Act. Doing so is strictly prohibited. As a result, any company still conducting business in the cannabis industry in international markets is exposed to many risks. The next section discusses risks. Be sure to seek legal counsel if you plan to expand operations abroad.

Legal and regulatory risk factors

A key, if not top risk for cannabusinesses, is legal and regulatory risk. Not complying with regulations and winding up on the wrong side of the law is serious business and serious trouble. On top of that, there are competitive, operational, reputational, and strategic risks to consider.

The top risks that you yourself must manage are

- **Regulatory:** Small cannabusinesses sell into and cater to a highly regulated niche market. This makes demand for your products or services uncertain. The gradual easing of laws also works the other way around.

As competitors grow in size, number, and complexity, you'll lose market share even if you're one of the first movers.

- **Barriers to entry:** Licensing is still a huge hurdle that you may have to overcome (especially if you're a grower, processor, or retailer where some provinces have retail license quotas), but there are low barriers to entry for new cannabusinesses, especially those companies that serve the ancillary marijuana market, which we discuss later in this chapter.

- **Large competitors:** Big Tobacco, Big Pharma, and Big Food are poised to steal away customers, even from the relative minnows but true innovators that people have come to know as small cannabusinesses.

- **Short supply:** Cannabis supply, at the time of writing, was a significant problem. You can't sell what you don't have. You can't support an ecosystem that suffers from frequent shortages. From a financial risk perspective, sure, strong demand and low supply equals profits. After all, shortages increase the per-gram price of cannabis. Yet, despite the rapid capacity expansion of many growers who anticipated the passing of legislation, most projects won't be fully operational until the end of 2020.

- **Long-term oversupply:** What goes down must come up. Although undersupply is a bit of a problem now, oversupply may be a problem down the road. Estimates from analysts suggest that four of the largest cannabis producers — Aurora Cannabis, Canopy Growth Corporation, Aphria, and the Green Organic Dutchman — are poised to collectively grow and produce 1.5 million kilograms by 2020, and grow even more beyond that time. On the bright side (from the perspective of entrepreneurs), perhaps this excess supply will be absorbed by foreign markets if and when exporting laws become clearer and more relaxed.

Government can definitely get in the way of recreational marijuana production, sale, and use. This risk is political. Political interference on hot-button issues like this can and ought to be expected. The issue is the nature and extent of the meddling. Given the recent legalization, industry momentum, and demand (read: votes), there is still some residual risk.

Finally, enforcement risks (enforcement is a good thing for the industry) are high, so you'd better operate a legitimate business. This means paying extra attention to avoiding certain behaviors and risks. For example, to steer clear of trouble, your cannabusiness must have zero tolerance for

- Distribution of marijuana to minors
- Profits from the sale of cannabis going to criminal enterprises
- Diverting marijuana from areas where it's legal to areas where it is not
- Government-authorized cannabis activity used as a cover for the trafficking of other illegal drugs or other illegal activity
- Violence and the use of firearms in the distribution of marijuana
- Drugged driving
- Growing marijuana on public lands and the related safety concerns

How to Get Clear on Your Big Product or Service Idea

Canadians today are witness to the birth of an entire industry. This environment of innovation, ideas, animal spirits, and change has given rise to many opportunities — both known and yet to be discovered. When you start a small business in any sector or industry within that sector, a unique idea that meets demand is obviously an essential and fundamental ingredient to reach small business success. As Chapter 3 explains, your business will be in deep trouble if you offer a product or service that no one wants or is interested in.

The next few sections give you some big-picture tips to brainstorm ideas.

Generate a unique cannabusiness idea

When you brainstorm ideas, it's useful to start at the top of the idea pyramid. Okay, maybe second from the top. If you already decided to jump into cannabusiness, you've already picked a sector — cannabis. The next step is to figure out the industry within that sector. For example, weed growth, distribution, and retail are core industry components of the broader cannabis sector, much like software and hardware are industries within the broader technology sector. Industries can be further divided into subsets and so on and so on. It's most helpful to start at the top of the idea pyramid and work your way to the bottom. It's not the only way to brainstorm, but it is logical and methodical.

If you're totally new to the sector, you'll likely think about dispensaries and grow ops if only because they're in the news a lot. However, the cannabis industry includes much more than that. Other cool ideas in the news include "bud and breakfasts," which are cannabis-friendly lodges and facilities. News is a good source of ideas.

You may want to brainstorm in terms of what you know best. For example, if you're into food or you have a background associated with restaurants, you may look into making a unique line of edibles. Again, at the time of this writing, legislation prohibited such edibles. But change is coming, and getting in front of change may give you first-mover advantage. Leverage your strengths.

 Be sure to check out the legal requirements first, preferably with the second opinion (or first) of legal counsel experienced in this sector. Cannabusiness entrepreneurs absolutely need to make sure that their idea is legally viable in addition to offering a compelling and unique product or service.

 If you prefer to dip your toes instead of diving in head first, a less risky type of small cannabusiness to launch is one that doesn't directly touch the "bud." When you look at the Cannabis Act, much of the regulations pertain to cannabis growers, processors, and retailers. This makes ancillary marijuana businesses an appealing option because they're less burdened with red tape and high taxes.

Consider start-up and ongoing costs

Start-up costs should be one of the first things you need to consider. The nature of the cannabusiness you're thinking about and extent of its size (staff, space, scope, and scale) are the real

drivers of start-up costs. Sure, it's great to start a vast cultivation operation that stretches to the horizon, but unless you
have access to a bank vault, it's not going to come cheap.

As you think of an idea, research its costs and compare
that cost and effort to your financial risk appetite. For example,
conventional wisdom and experience have been that start-up
and operational costs are significantly lower for infused product companies as compared to cultivators and larger retailers,
making profitability more likely and speedy. If the costs you
come up with are too scary, quickly move on to another brain-
storming session to generate other ideas.

Evidence to date points to a hung jury when it comes to
ancillary cannabusinesses. Companies that provide services
to the cannabis industry and its customers are thriving, with
almost half reporting meaningful profitability. On the other
hand, ancillary products (not services), as well as technology
firms, are still searching for a pot of gold in their pot-related
businesses. About a quarter of this group reports losing "some
or a lot of money." Why? Many of these companies must invest
a significant amount of money to get started, and they face stiff
competition once launched.

Understand your consumer base

When you come up with your idea, you'll have already thought
about your consumer base. Now you have to take a deeper

dive into understanding this base. It's vital to know exactly who is going to be interested in your products or services and to really understand their particular wants and needs.

When starting a cannabis business, two things are especially critical in addition to start-up costs and other considerations:

- Understanding the unique challenges of this sector and industries within the sector

- Understanding your consumer base and the unmet need you're satisfying for them

The cannabis industry is different from any industry you've ever worked in. The unique legal, regulatory, operational, financial, taxation, marketing, and reputational stigma elements of cannabusiness will take a big bite out of your profits and will siphon your attention away from the more fundamental and core elements of your business. Be aware of these unique challenges.

It's precisely because the legal cannabis space is becoming crowded that you need to have a targeted consumer segment to focus on. Know who your core consumers are and what they want from the products and services you plan to provide.

The cannabis ecosystem is very connected and interrelated. It's not the best place for a lone-wolf small business to be. Success is tied to the connectivity, relationships, and leadership that you and your cannabusiness will cultivate with the local cannabis community.

5

Figuring Out Finances

If you're starting a business, you need money. Maybe just a little bit, and maybe you already have it; maybe a lot, and you have to scout around for more. In any case, you need to know exactly how much money to hunt for, where to hunt for it, what you're going to have to do to bag it, and what risks you may have to take.

Your Business Needs Capital

You'll have to spend money so your business can begin operating. These are *start-up expenses* or *capital expenses*. For example, you'll need money to

- Acquire or protect the right to use an idea in your business.

- Identify the nature of your business — researching and developing your product, and doing market research (see Chapter 3). You'll also need money for your initial promotional activities (see Chapter 8).

- Set up your business as a legal entity (see Chapter 7). And while you're hanging out at the lawyer's, you'll need money for any additional work your lawyer does for you, such as preparing standard documents for your business to use. Not to favour lawyers over accountants, you'll also need money for initial advice and assistance from a certified accountant about the form of your business you choose and how best to structure it to keep accounting difficulties and taxes to a minimum.

- Buy equipment for your business.

- Locate your business in its own premises (see Chapter 7).

- Buy an existing business (like a franchise; see Chapter 3).

Table 5-1 helps you to add up the cost of everything related to startup.

If you're buying a business instead of building your own, your table of start-up expenses will look like Table 5-2.

Your initial capital (the money you already have for your business enterprise)	$
Fees for licensing a product to manufacture, use, or sell, or for patenting your own invention	$
Research and development of your product or service (Chapter 3)	$
Initial promotional activities (Chapter 8)	$
Legal and accounting fees for business setup	$
Purchase of equipment	$
Purchase price and legal fees if you intend to buy property for your business premises	$
Leasehold improvements and legal fees to review the lease, if you intend to rent business premises; or renovation costs if you set up a home office (Chapter 7)	$
Total new capital (add up initial capital plus the costs you've listed)	$
Total capital required (subtract initial capital from total new capital): This amount is how much you need but don't have at the moment	$

Table 5-1: *Start-Up Expenses for a Custom-Built Business*

Your initial capital (the money you already have to buy a business)	$
Purchase price of the business	$
Professional fees (lawyer, accountant, broker, valuator, and so on) associated with the purchase	$
Total new capital (add up initial capital plus the price of the business plus professional fees)	$
Total capital required (subtract initial capital from total new capital): This amount is how much you need but don't have at the moment	$

Table 5-2: *Start-Up Expenses If You Buy an Existing Business*

How Much Your Business Will Need to Operate

After you figure out the capital requirements of your business, you're still not ready to carry on business . . . at least not for very long. You also have to work out how much money you'll need to run the business on a day-to-day basis (actually a month-to-month basis). These are called *operating expenses*. After your business is generating a steady income, your revenues will cover all or most of your operating expenses. But until then, you'll need to borrow money to pay for such things as

- Salaries
- Lease or mortgage payments
- Utilities such as hydro, and water
- Telephone, fax, and Internet fees
- Insurance premiums
- Property taxes, if you own your business premises rather than rent them
- Ongoing professional fees (legal, accounting, advertising, publicity)
- Cost of running any vehicles

Projected expenses and revenues

For some of your operating expenses, you'll be able to write down a fairly accurate estimate from a supplier (such as a landlord or accountant or insurance agent). For others (such as utilities, and maybe salaries), you'll just have to guess.

After estimating your expenses, you have to estimate how much revenue you'll bring in to cover your expenses. This step will give you a better grasp of how much money you really need to borrow for monthly operations.

Projecting your expenses is easier than projecting your revenues. But you can make a guess at your revenues by making some assumptions. The usual assumptions are

- The number of customers or clients you'll get

- The average amount of each sale or transaction

 Multiply these two figures together to estimate sales. (Make a note to yourself about how you chose the figures you're using. You'll need to add that information as a footnote to your forecast of projected revenue and expenses.)

A forecast of revenue and expenses

The figures in the previous section get plugged into a forecast or projection of revenue and expenses. Take a look at Table 5-3.

Revenue		
Sales or revenues	$	
Other	$	
Total revenue		$
Expenses		
Salary of owner	$	
Salary of employee(s)	$	
Lease payments	$	
Advertising	$	
Insurance	$	
Utilities	$	
Telephone, fax, and Internet	$	
Legal costs	$	
Accounting services	$	
Vehicle operation and maintenance	$	
Other	$	
Total expenses		$
Net profit or loss (deduct total expenses from total revenue)		$

Table 5-3: *Forecast of Revenue and Expenses (for the First Year of Operation)*

Filling out this table gives you a reasonable idea of what your operating expenses will be for your first year of business, and whether you can expect that, by the end of the year, your revenues will cover your expenses, or that you'll be in the hole (and how deep the hole is).

Projected cash flow

Knowing how much money you need to operate your business isn't enough — you also have to know when you need the money. Revenue and expenses rarely match each other exactly, so you can't necessarily expect to be able to pay your expenses out of the revenue you're making. Your revenue may come in a lump once a year or a few times a year, whereas your expenses are likely to be fairly steady on a month-by-month basis.

By preparing a *cash flow statement* (a statement that shows the money going into and out of your business over time), you'll know when you may need bridge financing to keep the business afloat. This information is especially important during the first year or so of your business's existence, before revenue is steady or before you've been able to put aside some profits to operate the business between infusions of revenue.

Many of your expenses won't change from month to month (lease or mortgage payments, for example), and others may be predictable even though they change during the course of the year (a snow removal contract during the winter months, or salaries for extra staff during a busy season). But if you had trouble estimating your total annual revenue, you'll have even more trouble estimating how it will come in month by month. Give it a shot, though, taking into consideration that your monthly revenue will probably increase over the course of the first year as your business gets established.

Your business may have seasonal highs and lows, too. An accountant, for example, can probably expect a high just after income tax returns are filed and the bills go out for tax preparation; a business that sells cards and gifts can probably expect highs just before Christmas, Valentine's Day, and Mother's Day.

Table 5-4 doesn't have room for all 12 months plus an annual total, so it uses some representative months. (Fill in all 12 months when you prepare your cash flow statement.)

Filling out this table gives you some idea of how many months of the first year you'll need a loan to pay your operating expenses (from the cash flow line), and at what point your revenues will start reducing your need for a loan (from the cumulative cash flow line).

	Jan.	Feb.	...	Nov.	Dec.	Year
Revenue:						
Cash sales						
Receivables						
Total revenue						
Expenses:						
Salaries						
Lease						
Advertising						
Insurance						
Utilities						
Telephone						
Professional						
Total expenses						
Cash flow:						
(Subtract monthly expenses from monthly revenue. If the result is a negative number, put brackets around the number.)						
Cumulative Cash Flow						
(Move from left to right adding the previous month's cash flow to the following month. For January, you'll have the same number as for the January cash flow, but for February you'll add the cash flow numbers for January and February together; for March, you'll add January, February, and March together, and so on. Again, put brackets around negative numbers.)						

Table 5-4: *Projected Cash Flow Statement*

Sources of Financing for a Start-Up Operation

The previous sections help you to know, more or less, how much money you need to start up and run your business for the first year. So, where are you going to find that money? Generations of businesspeople have wondered the same thing, so you can turn to a standard list of sources of money. The sources include

- Personal assets
- Money from family and friends
- Borrowed money: Mortgage on a home or vacation property, commercial loans (capital and operating), and micro-credit loans
- Credit: Suppliers, customers
- Sale of accounts receivable
- Grants and loans from government
- Investment from external sources: Angel investor, venture capital company

That's a respectable-looking list — somewhere among all these possibilities, you should be able to find a buck or two.

The federal Innovation, Science, and Economic Development Canada website (www.ic.gc.ca) maintains a financing page that provides information on finding sources of funding and financial assistance. Click the Business tab, and then click the Grants and Financing tab to learn about various financing options including government grants and loans.

Mix-and-match financing

Most businesses need a combination of financing. For example, besides using personal assets and funds from family and friends to get started,

- To get equipment, a business might need a capital loan, a conditional sales agreement, or a lease.

- To get operating funds, a business might need a line of credit, payment in advance from customers and clients, or credit from suppliers.

- To make leasehold improvements, a business might need a capital loan.

So, you'll likely be dealing with several sources of financing. Be sure to read all the following sections carefully.

Personal assets

Most entrepreneurs start off using at least some of their own money. Look around and see what money you have handy — or what property you can turn into cash — to finance your business start-up. Keep in mind that you still need money to live on while you're getting your business off the ground. You're not going to be a very effective CEO if you're starving or sleeping on the street.

Personal assets include

- Money in bank accounts

- Bonds

- Stocks (But if they've increased in value since you acquired them, you'll have to declare a capital gain on your next income tax return and can end up taking a tax hit.)

- Registered Retirement Savings Plans, or RRSPs (But remember that you'll have to pay withholding taxes to the tax man and also add any amount you withdraw to your income for the year, which may attract more taxes.)

- Personal property or real property. (Property you can sell, such as vehicles, jewellery, collectibles, art, a vacation home . . . or even your real home. If property other than your real home — your principal residence — has increased in value since you acquired it, you'll have to declare a capital gain on your income tax return and may have to pay tax.)

Money from family and friends

Family and friends may be willing to lend money to you, or they may be willing to give it to you flat out. Think very carefully, however, before asking relatives and friends for money. If your business tanks and you can't repay them, they'll probably stop speaking to you. Then not only will you have no business, but no one to give you sympathy, either.

 If you do go ahead, make a formal arrangement with the lenders, for two reasons:

- So that they can get something back if you're successful or if you go bust (a document will provide the evidence they need to make a claim against your business as a creditor).

- So that they can't demand their money back just when you desperately need it.

Awkward moments aside, if the money or property is a gift, the giver should sign a document stating that the money or property is a gift and is yours absolutely to do with what you like. If the money is a loan, you should have a contract (a promissory note) with the lender setting out

- The amount of the loan

- The rate of interest payable on the loan (if any)

- The amount of each payment and the payment dates (a schedule of payments)

• The nature of the security, if any, the lender wants for the loan (*Security* is something the lender can take in exchange if the loan isn't repaid. It can include a mortgage against your home, or the taking of shares in your corporation, or a guarantee from someone else associated with you or the business that he or she will repay the loan if you don't.)

Money borrowed from commercial lenders

Commercial lenders are banks, trust companies, credit unions, *caisses populaires*, finance companies, and insurance companies. They've got lots of money . . . if you can just get your hands on it.

Many commercial lenders can also help you get access to funds from the Business Development Bank of Canada (www.bdc.ca) and from the federal government's Canada Small Business Financing (CSBF) program (www.ic.gc.ca/eic/site/csbfp-pfpec.nsf/eng/Home). Most small businesses starting up or operating in Canada are eligible for CSBF loans, as long as their estimated annual gross revenues don't exceed $5 million during the fiscal year in which they apply for a loan. As for the Business Development Bank of Canada, it does market itself as "the only bank exclusively devoted to entrepreneurs." Hold the bank to it.

Credit cards

If you need to borrow from a bank, your first thought may be to use your credit cards. It's easy — no application forms to fill out, no waiting, no business plan to prepare, no intimidating interview with a bank manager. You may even have a high enough limit on your card(s) to get as much money as you need.

Absolutely don't use your credit cards! The interest rate on credit cards is astronomical compared to the interest rate you'll pay if you borrow in a more businesslike fashion — probably at least double and maybe triple. This chapter has better suggestions.

A mortgage on your home or vacation property

If you own real property and it isn't already mortgaged to the hilt, you can borrow against that property by taking out a mortgage. If you're thinking of mortgaging property, consider these factors:

- **What is the property worth?** Will mortgaging it get you as much money as you need? You probably won't be able to borrow its full unmortgaged value.

- **Is the property already mortgaged?** If it is, you may not have enough equity (unmortgaged value) in the property to get as big a loan as you need.

- **Do you need someone else's legal consent to mortgage the property?** You do if you have a co-owner. Even if you're the only owner, if you're married, in most provinces your spouse will have to give consent to the transaction before you'll get any money (sometimes even if it's not your family home that you're borrowing against).

- **Can you afford to lose the property if your business fails?** If you default on your loan (don't pay it back on time), the lender has the right to take the property — and either keep it or sell it to cover your unpaid loan. Don't kid yourself for a second. Banks can be ruthless and will sell your property from under you in a second. (If it's sold, you'll get the excess over the outstanding amount of the loan plus legal fees.)

Business loans

If you're borrowing because you need money to purchase capital assets for your business, you'll apply for a *capital loan*. If you're borrowing because you need money to cover the ongoing costs of running your business, you'll apply for an *operating loan*. You can get either kind of loan from a commercial lender. But choose a branch that regularly handles small business clients, if you can find one — if the branch staff are only used to making deposits and withdrawals, they won't know what to do with you . . . and they might show you the door.

Banks, most credit unions, and many trust, loan, and insurance companies can make a loan under the CSBF program for capital expenses, including the purchase or improvement of real property, leasehold improvements, and the purchase or improvement of equipment. The federal government partially guarantees CSBF loans, so lenders are more willing to lend, and owners don't have to provide personal assets as security.

The amount of money the lender gives is called the *principal* or *principal amount* of the loan. The amount the borrower pays for the use of the money is called *interest*. (You're not going to find an interest-free loan if you deal with anyone other than your mother.) Interest is calculated as a percentage of the principal. If you're charged *simple interest* on the loan, you pay interest only on the principal you've borrowed. So, if you borrowed $100,000 at 10 percent, you'd owe $10,000 in interest per year.

But commercial lenders charge *compound interest* on a loan if the terms of repayment stretch past the time the interest is actually due. Compound interest is interest on the principal and on the interest owing. When you're charged compound interest, you end up with a higher interest rate (the *effective interest rate*) than the rate you're quoted (the *nominal interest rate*). And the more often the interest is *compounded* or *calculated*, the higher the real interest rate.

Interest can be compounded on any basis the lender chooses — daily, weekly, monthly, semi-annually, or annually. If you borrowed $100,000 at 10 percent compounded monthly, your real interest rate would actually be 10.47 percent. And in commercial loans, unlike consumer loans, the lender doesn't have to tell the borrower the total amount of interest payable over the life of the loan (the cost of borrowing).

You'll likely take out either a *term loan* or a *line of credit.* Capital loans are usually term loans. Operating loans usually come in the form of a line of credit. If you have a term loan, the lender sets a schedule for regular repayment of principal and interest.

If you have a line of credit, also known as *overdraft protection,* the lender (which is normally your bank) tops up your business account if you don't have enough in the account to cover a cheque. Then when you make a deposit to your business account, the money is automatically applied to pay down the loan. You may also be required to make regular payments or make a deposit to the account within a fixed period of time to cover the overdraft.

A line of credit is usually a *demand loan,* which means that the lender can demand payment in full at any time, not just after you've missed a payment. However, if you make your payments on time, demand will not be made — unless you do something to lead the lender to believe that your business is in trouble. The lender also usually requires you to sign blank promissory notes, which it fills in as the line of credit goes up.

The promissory note provides evidence of what you owe, and the lender can also sue you on the note if you don't pay the loan.

Lenders don't take for granted that borrowers will pay up on schedule — or ever. They know they could sue the borrower for failing to pay, but they also know that suing someone is expensive and time-consuming, and even if they win the lawsuit, collecting the money is often difficult. So, to make life easier for themselves, lenders usually require borrowers to give *security* or *collateral*. When a borrower gives security, he legally gives the lender the right to take specified property from the borrower if the borrower doesn't make his payments. The lender usually sells the property to pay off the loan. Typically, lenders take security on such property as

- **Real estate:** Security will take the form of a *collateral mortgage* or *charge* or, in Quebec, a *hypothec*.

- **Equipment and other non-land assets:** Security may take the form of a *chattel mortgage,* known in some provinces as a *specific security agreement.*

- **Accounts receivable, also known as *book debts*, which is money that customers or clients owe the borrower:** Security can take the form of an *assignment of accounts receivable,* which gives the lender the right to collect debts owing to you if you default on your loan.

- **Inventory:** The lender may be able to take security under *s. 427* of the federal *Bank Act* if you are borrowing from a chartered bank.

If you have a capital loan, the lender will probably want security over the capital property (real estate or equipment) you're buying. If you have a line of credit or overdraft protection, the lender may want security over your business's accounts receivable and inventory.

Other forms of security that a lender might ask for include

- **A general security agreement:** This gives a lender security over almost all of the borrower's existing and future assets (usually excluding real property, but including equipment, vehicles, machinery, inventory, and accounts receivable).

- **A debenture:** This is much like a general security agreement, except that only a corporation can give a debenture as security for a loan, and a debenture usually includes real property, as well as other assets.

- **A pledge of shares (or of bonds or debentures) that are the personal property of the borrower or a guarantor:** For example, if the borrower is a corporation, the lender may want a pledge of shares of the corporation from the shareholders who have guaranteed the loan. Then, if the borrower does not repay the loan, the lender can take control of the corporation.

And lenders don't always stop at taking security. Sometimes they want (instead of or in addition to security) a *guarantee*. A guarantee is a promise by someone other than the borrower that if the borrower doesn't pay up, the *guarantor* (the person or business giving the guarantee) will repay the loan. For example, if the borrower is a corporation — especially a corporation that doesn't have much by way of assets — the lender might ask for a guarantee from the individuals associated with the corporation, such as the shareholders or the directors. A bank can also ask for security from the guarantor, such as a *collateral mortgage* on the guarantor's home.

If the borrower does not meet the lender's criteria to receive a loan, the lender may be willing to go ahead with the loan if someone who does meet the criteria agrees to co-sign the loan. Unlike a guarantor, a *co-signor* can be required to repay the loan even if the borrower is capable of repaying the loan himself.

Micro-credit funds

Micro-credit is a small loan (usually only a few thousand dollars), available to individuals with a low income, to help them start up a very small business. (They're often targeted toward young people, or women, or new immigrants, or people with disabilities; they may also be targeted toward a restricted geographical area.) Micro-credit can be used for capital investment or operating funds. Micro-credit may be made available by an independent operation, as part of an integrated community economic development program, or by a micro-finance program of a commercial lender. They often offer, besides money, business courses and networking opportunities.

Credit from suppliers and clients

Maybe you didn't realize you could put your customers and suppliers to work for you as lenders.

Suppliers

If you're buying equipment or machinery, you may be able to finance the purchase through a loan from the vendor, a conditional sales agreement, or a lease. The vendor will probably want a down payment and security (for example, a chattel mortgage if the vendor is loaning you the money), and will want to be repaid on a regular schedule, as would a commercial lender.

If you're buying inventory or supplies, you may be able to get financing through a credit arrangement. Suppliers may offer 30, 60, or 90 days to pay, with a discount if payment is made within a shorter time. (Two problems exist here: First, because you're a start-up without a credit history, suppliers might not want to extend credit and might instead want cash on delivery from you. Second, the effective interest rate you pay on the money you're "borrowing" by not taking the discount is high — in the range of 20 percent to 30 percent or more.)

Suppliers might also sometimes offer a loan, or else a sale on *consignment* (you don't pay the supplier until a customer purchases a consigned item). If you buy inventory on credit, the supplier may want to take security in the form of a *purchase money security interest* (in other words, the supplier takes security on the items purchased on credit).

Customers

You may well be able to get your clients or customers to finance the work you do for them by getting them to pay a deposit or *retainer* (that's what professionals call a deposit) and/or installment payments as you do the work (instead of waiting to be paid when everything's finished).

Sale of accounts receivable

You can sell your recent accounts receivable at a discount for instant cash. This is called *factoring* and it's more expensive than borrowing — it can be a lot more expensive — but you don't have to show that your business has revenue and you don't have to put up security. The factor pays you a percentage of the value of your receivables immediately, collects the receivables, deducts fees, and sends you the balance. (Depending on your arrangement with the factor, your customers don't need to know they're dealing with a factor instead of with your business.)

The initial percentage you get from the factor will depend on things like the value of the receivables, number of customers, and creditworthiness of the customers — it can run anywhere from about 90 percent down to 30 percent. In "recourse" factoring, the factor can look to you to cover any bad debts, while in "nonrecourse" factoring (which is, naturally, more expensive) bad debts are the factor's risk. Factoring is available from factoring companies, finance companies, and some banks. It's traditionally used in the apparel, textile, carpet, and furniture industries, but it's not restricted to those industries.

Government loans and grants

You, too, may be able to snarf up some money from the public trough to start and run your business! You can find lots of government assistance programs — to browse, go to the Innovation, Science, and Economic Development Canada site (www.ic.gc.ca), click the Business tab, and then click the Grants and Financing tab for information on government grants and loans. You can search for financing available throughout Canada, or restrict your search to financing available in your province.

For example, these sources may provide you with some repayable or even non-repayable money for your business:

- The National Research Council (www.nrc-cnrc.gc.ca/eng/irap), if you need to research and develop a new technological product or service

- Canada Council for the Arts (www.canadacouncil. ca), if your business involves artistic creation (like writing, painting, music, performance)

- Industry Canada (www.ic.gc.ca), which may provide grants or loans for various business initiatives

Arm's length investment

For some businesses, a start-up loan isn't much use. If you take out a loan, you have to pay it back — usually beginning right away — and your business, even though it has fantastic prospects over the next few years, won't be able to generate cash revenues for some time *and* it needs a cash infusion (perhaps a big one) to get started at all.

So, maybe what you need is *seed financing* or *seed capital* from an angel investor or a venture capital firm, rather than a loan from a lender.

Seed capital provides money for business activities such as the following:

- Proving that an idea or invention actually works in practice as well as it does in theory (*proof of concept*)

- Protecting intellectual property (usually through a patent)

- Completing a prototype (*working model*) of a product or invention

- Doing market research

- Creating strategic partnerships with other businesses or with potential customers
- Hiring experienced managers for the business
- Creating a business plan (see Chapter 6)
- Hunting down even more capital that's required to start the business operating

The great majority of start-up businesses don't need seed capital for these kinds of things. And even start-ups that do aren't that likely to get outside investment in the business. Most requests for investment get rejected either because the business has limited financial prospects or because the managers of the business don't have the necessary skills to run the business successfully. But the following sections go on and briefly tell you about outside investors anyway.

Angel investors

If you go around talking about angel investors, chances are most people will think you've been out in the sun too long. You'll get the same kind of reaction as if you mentioned that aliens are broadcasting messages to you through the fillings in your teeth.

Angel investors actually do exist, however. They're individuals, often successful businesspeople, who want to invest their own money in promising new businesses, usually in the same field the angel comes from (many or most come from a high-tech background), and usually in businesses in their own geographic area.

Angels usually invest an amount in the range of $10,000 to $150,000, although some may go as high as $500,000 or more if they have the money and they really like the business's prospects. Besides providing money, angel investors also take an interest in the running of the business. Because they're experienced, they may be able to proactively help you find customers and sell your product, put you in touch with suppliers and professional advisors, and prepare you and your business to hunt for the next round of financing.

Angels are looking for a good return on their investment in your business — typically 30 percent compound annual returns. Not many business owners even plan for their business to grow that aggressively, much less are capable of making it happen. Angels are also looking for *equity* in (a share in the value of) your business and the right to be involved in major decisions and to get frequent status reports.

Heaven? Sure, but maybe closer than that. Network in your own business community and ask around about angel investors. Ask your lawyer or accountant. Some business incubators help to connect client companies with angel investors. Or you can try the National Angel Capital Organization (www.angelinvestor.ca).

If you find an angel, he or she won't necessarily be interested in investing in your kind of business. Learn as much as you can about an angel before approaching him or her, and customize your pitch to match the angel's interests.

Venture capital

Venture capital is money that's available for risky investments with a good chance of getting a high return on the investment. Over $12 billion in venture capital is floating around in the Canadian economy at the moment, and in the past few years venture capitalists (VCs) have poured about $2 billion per year into businesses, mostly in the technology, life sciences, clean tech, and agricultural sectors. However, that doesn't mean that you'll be able to get any of it. VCs are ridiculously fussy about whom they give their money to.

VCs are typically looking for three things:

- **A large market opportunity** — one that will provide very high returns within a fairly short time, about five to seven years

- **Good managers** — or at least one good and committed manager who will be able to recruit a strong management team

- **A strategic plan about building the business** — one that includes a lucrative exit strategy for the VCs

Like angel investors, VCs offer money, management expertise, and connections — to other money, to professional advisors like lawyers and accountants, and to suppliers and potential customers.

To put this section into perspective, note that VCs are also known, affectionately of course, as vulture capitalists. What they usually want is

- **At least a 25 percent return on investment** — and they're really thrilled at the prospect of getting a 300 percent to 500 percent return (a *home run*).

- **Significant ownership of the business** — they usually want 20 percent or more of the business's equity, plus their own director(s) on the board of directors.

- **A lucrative exit strategy within five to seven years.** Exit strategies include the following: an *initial public offering* (IPO), sale of the business to another corporation, a company buyback (the business or business owners buy back the VC's share of the corporation), or a write-off of the investment (as lost money) . . . although clearly this is not "lucrative."

 Venture capital firms are very easy to find. You can get a list of them by going to the Canadian Venture Capital and Private Equity Association website (www. cvca.ca), and from there you can link to the website of each association member. You can get contact information, as well as some information about the interests and expectations of each member, from the member's website. Finding VCs, of course, does not necessarily mean getting money from them.

Crowdfunding

You've likely heard about crowdfunding, and you may be wondering what it's all about, whether it's right for your business idea, and its legality. *Crowdfunding* occurs when a person or organization raises money over the Internet by soliciting a group of people for individual contributions. There are various forms of crowdfunding, but the main ones simply seek donations. Crowdfunding is also used by companies and nonprofit organizations to raise capital.

If you see crowdfunding as an option to explore and you want to actually pursue this avenue, you need to provide investors with some information such as an offering document, financial statements, and periodic updates about how the money you raised is being used. It requires time, thought, and effort. Regulators will be watching, too, so it's important to know whether your province allows crowdfunding and, if so, what the rules are.

Crowdfunding in Canada is mostly regulated at the provincial level. An in-depth discussion of this form of financing is beyond the scope of this book, but you can check out an excellent source of information at

www.crowdfundontario.ca, which is geared more toward Ontario investors but offers an excellent overview of the industry as a whole. From there, check out the links to the Ontario Securities Commission's pronouncements and requirements over businesses engaged in crowdfunding.

Another great site, geared toward businesses exploring crowdfunding options in British Columbia, is www.bcsc.bc.ca/For_Companies/Private_

Placements/Crowdfunding. This website has useful guides, as well as links to *funding portals* — the online platforms actually used to make your case and raise and collect money. Just Google the term *crowdfunding* and the name of your province to learn more.

Check with security regulator websites such as www.osc.gov.on.ca to stay on top of rapidly changing

regulations over crowdfunding. There are risks and penalties involved if you run afoul of these regulations — all geared toward protecting investors. Be sure to check with your legal counsel before proceeding with this route.

How to Apply for Money

Be aware that before you approach a commercial lender, a government granting agency, an angel investor, or a venture capital firm (and maybe even members of your family whom you're tapping for love money), you'll have to show what you plan to do with any money you get, and why you should be trusted with it. The more money you want, the more work you'll have to do when you apply for it. The most work you'll be asked to do is prepare a business plan (see Chapter 6). But for a loan that's not too large (say, less than $35,000 to $50,000), and assuming that over the years you've built a good credit rating, you'll probably just be asked to fill out an application form provided by the lender.

6

Writing a Business Plan That Gets You Money

Sometimes preparing an application to get money involves filling out a form created by the lender, and sometimes it involves preparing a business plan. Most of this chapter focuses on a formal business plan because preparing a business plan is a lot more difficult than filling out an application form.

What Goes into a Business Plan

Books and even chapters about business plans are often incredibly detailed and seem to be written for existing businesses that are looking to expand and need huge amounts of money.

They're intimidating, and by the time you get to the end of the book or chapter, you feel like writing a business plan is pointless because you don't have an MBA and you don't understand the marketing and accounting jargon.

Don't twist yourself into knots about writing a business plan. Although almost every book or article you read about creating a business plan will tell you a somewhat different way to set up the plan, all business plans contain the same — quite understandable — basic information.

A full-scale business plan

 If a lender is looking for the whole shebang, business-plan-wise, here's the core information required:

- The amount of money you want from the person who's reading the business plan and what you're going to do with it.

- A description of what your business does, and a description of the industry your business is part of.

- An explanation about why your business can compete successfully, and your strategy for competing (that is, for marketing your product or service).

- A description of how your business runs or will run on a day-to-day basis, including information about the business's managers.

- The financial information about your business, including projections about revenue and expenses (as a start-up you won't have much financial history), and also about your personal financial status and individual financial commitment to the enterprise — so the lender or investor can decide whether investing is safe. A lender or investor will expect to be paid back out of profits of the business or (if the business doesn't generate enough profits) out of the sale of what the business owns . . . and/or what you own.

A mini business plan

If the lender doesn't want to know every last detail about your business (and who can say whether the lenders who do want to know every detail actually read the business plan from cover to cover?), you need to prepare only a short version. A mini business plan would cover any given topic more briefly, and it might include only the following information:

- The amount of money you want from the lender and what you'll do with it

- The name and address of the business, the form of the business, and how long it's been established

- The nature of your business, and what its goals are (essentially the five Ws: who, what, when, where, and why)

- A basic analysis of your market and competition
- The financial statements (also including a *pro forma* projected balance sheet, income statement, and statement of cash flows with assumptions)

A Statement of How Much You Want (Your Objective)

You should say right up front how much money you want and what you're going to do with it. You should also say right up front how this money will increase the profits or value of the business so that the loan can be repaid or the investment can provide a return.

No, you're not being rude or pushy by saying what you want. You'll save your potential lender or investor time and annoyance. No one with money wants to plod through pages of information without knowing beforehand why they're plodding. They'll want to assess what you want against what you have — and against what they have to offer — from the very beginning of your plan.

A Description of Your Business

A business plan describes your business, and how your business fits into the larger industry it's part of.

Your product or service

Start with what your business does — what product it manufactures or sells or what service it provides.

For example, if you're firing up a bakery operation, you'll describe the baked goods you're going to produce and your potential customers. If you're setting up a bookkeeping practice, you'll describe the services you plan to offer and to whom.

If your business has an intellectual property component — for example, if you're manufacturing a product that's patented or whose design is registered as an industrial design, or you're distributing or selling a product under a licence agreement or marketing a product under a trademark — then your plan should describe the status of protection of the product or service. For instance, if your product or method is patented, say so and mention its patent number, or if a patent has been applied for, say that a patent application is pending; if you're distributing a patented product, talk briefly about the licence agreement you have.

For a business that needs money to start manufacturing a product, you should be prepared to show a potential lender or investor working drawings and designs of the product.

The goals of your business

While your immediate goal is to get your business set up, you presumably also have other goals on the way to success. An investor would like to know where you're headed. So, your plan should outline

- Your short-term goals
- Your long-term plans

In the case of the bakery, for example, your short-term goal might be to produce ten dozen loaves of bread per day within a month of starting the operation and distribute them through five local independent food stores. A longer-term goal might be to produce 100 dozen loaves per day and distribute them through a grocery chain with stores around your city. Your ultimate goal (for the moment) might be to expand your baking operation to the point that it supplies bread for the grocery chain throughout the province; or it might be to franchise your bakery and sell franchises across the country.

If you think your business might attract a lot of interest from the world at large (and not just from your doting family and satisfied customers) and will need a large amount of invested money to expand and function properly, your long-term goal might be to become a publicly traded company. Publicly traded companies are able to raise money by offering their shares to the public through a stock exchange.

If you think your business is likely to be of great interest to one or more large corporations in the industry, and that a large corporation would show its interest via a nice fat offer to buy you out, your long-term goal might be to sell your business to a larger business.

Your business within the industry

Your business won't be operating in isolation. Even if you haven't thought about it that way, it's part of some fairly large-scale industry. Your bakery is part of the baked goods industry, your bookkeeping practice is in a small corner of the accounting industry, your computer program for hunting down certain kinds of information on the Internet is part of the computer software industry. The lender or investor you approach may not know much about the industry at all and will need background information to make a decision.

 So, you need to write a short profile of the industry. To do this you'll have to conduct some research by contacting industry associations, or reading industry publications, or searching for newspaper and magazine articles, or going through Statistics Canada data at `www.statcan.gc.ca/eng`. Chapter 2 gives you some ideas about doing your research.

Include some of the following information in your profile:

- **The size of businesses in the industry:** Some businesses are mainly made up of large multinational corporations, like the pharmaceutical industry; some are mainly made up of national corporations, like the Canadian banking industry . . . although you're probably not thinking of starting up a bank; others may have a mix of large and small businesses, like the legal and accounting industries; and some mostly consist of small businesses, like the personal services industry.

- **The total volume of sales in the industry and the total value of sales:** You're just going to have a small piece of the pie to start with, but do show that the pie is nice and big.

- **Any legislation, regulations, and standards that apply to the industry's products or services:** For example, the manufacture of food and drugs is heavily regulated by the federal government; travel agencies are regulated by provincial governments; cafés are regulated and inspected by municipal governments.

- **Trends in the industry:** It might be growing, or shrinking, or shifting its focus from certain products or services to others; or it might be facing stricter government regulation, or it might be about to be deregulated.

- **The main challenges and problems the industry faces:** Is it being forced to compete globally instead of nationally? Is it losing customers because it isn't meeting changing customer needs? Has it priced its goods or services out of the larger marketplace? Is it sluggish because it hasn't upgraded old infrastructure?

- **The future of the industry:** Will it stay much as it is but expand — or contract? Will it change significantly in response to consumer demand or new legislation?

By the way, don't make this stuff up. Making it up is easier and more fun, true, but it's a bad move. You'll look lightminded and untrustworthy if anyone finds out.

 And because you're not making it up, you should footnote facts and opinions that you state to show their source. If a lender or investor wants more information about the industry, he, she, or it should be able to locate your references.

After you've finished your industry profile, you have to discuss how your business fits into the industry. Are you going to create a product that will revolutionize the industry . . . or even make it obsolete? Are you going to take advantage of a gap and expand your business to become a major player? Are you going to quietly but competently fill a little niche?

How will industry trends affect your business's chance of success? How will your business meet the industry's challenges? How will your business fit into the industry's future that you've projected? This section gives you quite a mental workout! But preparing it makes you reflect on a lot of points that are important to your business success.

Why your business can compete successfully

After you describe your business world, you have to show that you can survive in it by competing successfully. In trying to figure out how well you'll be able to compete, you have to consider both the market for your product or your service, and your competition in the marketplace. Chapter 3 takes you through the process of developing a product or service and researching its market and its competition.

Your market

You need to know a reasonable amount about the market for your product or service so that you can

- Identify your target market for the product or service.
- Identify your portion of the total target market — probably not the total market, at least not to begin with.
- Identify marketing strategies (covering things such as prices, distribution, and business promotion).

Your target market

You can determine your target market in different ways. One is geography. Your target market may be the people (or businesses) within a geographic area. For example, if you run a retail business, you may see your target market as the people who live within walking distance or a short driving distance of your store. If you're distributing a product, you may have a distribution agreement with the manufacturer that allows you to distribute the product within your province or within a region (for example, the Maritime provinces, or the Vancouver area, or specified towns in northern Ontario). If you're the sole manufacturer of a product that's in demand (say, a Hula-Hoop during a Hula-Hoop craze) your geographic market might be the entire country or the entire continent.

Another way of determining your target market is by the characteristics of your customers or clients — for example, sex, age, interests, needs, and/or income level if your customers or clients are individuals; the kind of business and/or annual sales if your customers are other businesses.

Yet another way to view the market is in terms of its behavior. Behavioral market segmentation is a human-centered approach that segments your target market based on what your customers or clients actually do. For example, this form of segmentation considers how your customer base purchases certain types of products or services. Do they prefer online or bricks-and-mortar storefronts? Are customers repeat customers? At what time of day do they prefer to shop?

This type of market analysis uses available data, observation, and focus groups to distinguish a market by its behavior.

Your share of the target market

Besides figuring out who or what your target market is, you have to try to estimate what share of the target market your competitors hold and what share you can capture. This is guesswork unless you've got very few competitors. As an example, if you open a convenience store in a residential area where no other stores are located, you've got a good chance of getting a very big share of the target market (which is the inhabitants of the residential area). But — to take an example from the opposite end of the spectrum — if you're planning to sell T-shirts over the Internet (a huge total market), you may never be able to estimate your market share or a competitor's with anything approaching accuracy because many businesses are competing in a fickle market.

 If you're looking for a large sum of money, consider having a professional marketing study done to examine in detail the size of the market, the existing competitors in the market, and the market share your business might expect to capture.

Your marketing strategy

A lot of details go into identifying a marketing strategy. These details include

- **Your planned method(s) of selling and/or distributing your product or service:** Are you going to sell directly to the end user, or are you going to go through a third party (such as a manufacturer's agent or a distributor or a retailer, if you're a manufacturer)? If you already have contracts or partnerships with individuals or businesses or governments who are going to buy or distribute your product or service, mention them here.

- **Your location (if it affects marketing):** Your location is important if, for example, you're a retail store or service relying on walk-in customers, or if you provide a product that can be shipped only short distances to customers, or if you need to project an image to customers that can be achieved in only a certain area. Canadian wine coming from the Niagara region would be an example of the latter. Location isn't particularly important if you provide a service or product without needing face-to-face contact with your customers or clients. For example, running a call centre operation from an industrial plaza in the middle of nowhere is fine . . . as long as you can get workers to go there.

- **Your strategy for promoting the product:** This covers things like your business image, your advertising message, your public relations plan (if any), your sales strategy, and finding and keeping customers.

How are you going to present your business? Are you going to package it around a logo or trademark? Are you going to build it around a concept (such as one-stop errand running if you're starting up a personal assistant business) or a special product? Are you going to promote it as an essential for your target market (such as a business district spa for businesswomen)?

What's your advertising message, and your method and budget for getting the message out? Methods might include TV and radio spots; social media and other sites like Facebook, Twitter, blogs, and podcasts; newspaper ads; billboards and signs; flyers distributed around neighbourhoods or to local businesses — or even just word of mouth. The method should be appropriate to the target market and to the image you want your business to project.

Do you have a plan for approaching the media (in the hope that they'll write about you or interview you on TV news or a business program or a lifestyle show) and organizing events to attract media and/or customer attention? Media approaches might include press releases, contacts with acquaintances or friends of friends, or cold calls.

How are you going to set your basic price? (Generally speaking, it should be high enough to cover your costs of providing the product or service and earn you a profit, and low enough that your competitors are not underpricing you. Refer to Chapter 3 for more about pricing your product or service.) What other pricing procedures are you going to use to attract customers and clients? (Possibilities include gifts, coupons, or two-for-one offers; special sales to groups; or special rates for large purchases.)

What's your plan for coming up with leads to find new customers and clients? (Tried-and-true methods include advertising, arranging for other individuals and businesses to refer clients to you, and buying customer lists.) Are you going to make presentations to prospective clients or customers? (What will the content of the presentation be, and how will you jazz it up to give it impact?) How are you going to satisfy the customers you do get? (Think about a returns policy, guarantees, and product service provided on the premises.)

Your competitors

You need to know your market, but you also need to know your competitors. If you can't beat them at their own game, that will be the end of you.

In this part of your business plan, you'll

- **Fearlessly and transparently name your competitors.** Keep in mind, though, you're talking about your competitors in your target market and not all the competitors in the total market. If you're starting a dog walking business, your competitors aren't every personal service provider in the province, or even every dog walker in the city, just the dog walkers in the neighbourhood you plan to service.

- **Describe the similar products or services available from the competitors.** What are the strong points about the competing products or services, and what are the weak points? What do they do better than anyone else to distinguish themselves? What problems or vulnerabilities exist with the competition's product or services?

- **Explain why customers will buy the product or service from you instead of something similar from the competition.** Describe the strengths of your product or service.

Strong points of either the competitors' businesses or your business might include:

- Higher quality of services or product
- Innovative nature of the product or service (being the first to provide a product or service can give the provider

a competitive edge — but keep in mind that the first provider isn't necessarily the best provider)

- Lower cost of services or product
- Better distribution system
- Better management
- Better customer service — efficient, fast, friendly
- Better service guarantees that accompany the product
  or service
- A more convenient location
- Established base of loyal customers or clients
- Loyalty of customers or clients to a particular brand
- Access to a client/customer base that hasn't been
  tapped yet

Weaknesses are the flip side of these matters — such as
higher cost of the product, poorer quality of the service, less
convenient location, and so on.

Don't overdo describing your competitors' strengths
or your own weaknesses. You don't want to deep-six
your business proposal by presenting the competition
as unbeatable or you as a lost sheep among the coy-
otes. But you do want your potential investor to know
that you've taken an objective look at the market and
your chances of turning a good profit.

A List of References

You're exhausted, but you're not finished. As a final touch, a lender or investor might like to know more about your business reputation (or if you don't have a business reputation yet, your personal reputation) — but not from you. So be prepared to provide, if asked, the names of two or three people whom the lender or investor could speak to — for example, your bank branch manager if you've dealt with him or her for some time, or other businesspeople you've dealt with over the years (probably best not to name your competitors here . . . or your mother). If you've never been in business for yourself before, you could name an employer or a customer or client you worked with.

 Ask your references for permission before you give their names. At the very least, you don't want them to be taken by surprise when a lender calls up for a chat about you.

If your business venture revolves around marketing a new technology (say, new computer software or hardware), a lender or investor would probably like to have the names of a couple of people who know the field and who can give an opinion about the commercial potential of your technology. Again, avoid giving the name of a competitor.

Help for Your Business Plan

This chapter shows just how much hard work goes into a business plan, and no one would blame you if you want some help. Well, help is out there — some of it free, some of it for a price.

 You can purchase business plan software, such as Business Plan Pro (www.paloalto.com/business-plan-software), and you can access more than 500 sample business plans online at www.bplans.com.

 You can also get free templates, writing guides, and sample business plans from the websites of various business organizations:

- The Business Development Bank of Canada provides business plan templates at www.bdc.ca/en/articles-tools/entrepreneur-toolkit/templates-business-guides/pages/business-plan-template.aspx.

- Scotiabank has the Scotia Plan Writer, an interactive business planning tool, at www.scotiabank.com/ca/en/small-business/expertise-insight/business-plan.html.

- Community Business Development Corporations has an online business plan at www.cbdc.ca/en/ resources/how-to-write-a-business-plan.
- Futurpreneur Canada (www.futurpreneur.ca/en) supports aspiring business owners ages 18 to 39 and has an interactive business plan writer.

And if you don't feel like doing this all by yourself — just you and the software — you can go to your accountant. Your accountant can, at a minimum, put together the financials for your business plan after talking to you about your business and what you're planning to do with it.

You can also hire a consultant who can write a business plan for you — but expect to drop several thousand dollars for this service. You'll want to use a consultant who specializes in your business field.

You can find consultants (you can likely find consultants galore!) by asking your business acquaintances, or approaching your provincial, municipal, or regional economic development office for suggestions. You can also get in touch with a university business school — MBA students run assistance programs and will work with you on a business plan for a modest fee.

7

Other Important Considerations

Before you can start your business, you need a vehicle for carrying on your business — a "form of business" or a "business organization." Only a few forms of business exist, and this chapter takes you around to each one of them and helps you kick the tires. After you've looked at all of them and thought about your own business circumstances, you can decide which form of business is right for you and then make other important decisions about location and insurance.

Should You Go Alone or Take on a Copilot?

You'll often get asked, "What's your business?" But right now, this chapter asks, "Who's your business?" Is your business you and only you? Is it you and a pal? You and a group?

If your new business is a team effort, you can skip to the later section "Should You Incorporate?" now. If your new business is a one-person show, stick around and read this section.

 Certainly, being the only owner of a business has its advantages. Here are just a few of them:

- The profits of the business will be yours alone.

- You have the only say in what the business does, and you don't need anyone else's agreement to do what you want to do.

- Setting up a business with just one owner is usually easier, faster, and cheaper.

But here are reasons that you might want to, or have to, work with a co-owner:

- You may want someone else to share the financial risks of the business with you.

- You may want company — being in business all by yourself can be lonely.

- You may need someone else to provide skills or knowledge that you don't have.

- You may want someone to share the workload.

If you're now considering sharing ownership of your business with someone else, you should consider these questions:

- Are you capable of working well with a co-owner (and especially with any particular co-owner you have in mind)?

- Is the business likely to be able to generate enough revenue to support two (or more) owners?

- Does the business have roles for two (or more) owners to play?

- Does your potential co-owner have skills and knowledge that will add to yours (instead of having no useful skills and knowledge, or having the same skills and knowledge as you)?

 Ultimately, the reason you decide to go on alone or take a copilot with you should be that it will give your business a better chance of success.

Should You Incorporate?

"Should I incorporate?" is a very common first question that entrepreneurs ask, whether they're working alone or in a team. But it's not the *right* first question. It can't be answered in a vacuum. And before you even ask the question, you need to know about the alternatives to incorporation.

What are your options?

When you ask whether you should incorporate, what you're really asking is, "What form of business organization should I choose?" You have choices, and the choices available to you depend on whether your business will have only one owner, or two or more owners.

If you will be the only owner of the business, your choices are

- To operate as a sole proprietor
- To operate as a corporation that is owned by you

If two or more people will own the business, your choices are

- To operate as a partnership
- To operate as a corporation that is owned by you and your co-owner(s)

What's the difference?

The main distinction between a business that's incorporated and one that's not is that an incorporated business is a legal being separate from the owner of the business. So, if you incorporate your business, your personal assets (property owned by you personally) and the assets of the corporation (property owned by the business) are separate. Your personal debts (money owed by you personally) and the debts of the corporation (money owed by the business) are also separate. In theory, then, your personal assets can't be seized to pay the debts of the business.

What many people don't realize is that, in practice, keeping the business debts of your corporation away from your personal assets is not always possible. Many people are also unaware that you can protect your personal assets without incorporating your business.

Here are two other main differences between an incorporated and an unincorporated business:

- The profits of a corporation are taxed differently by the Canada Revenue Agency (CRA) than the profits of a business operated as a sole proprietorship or partnership.

- The amount of paperwork increases greatly when you're setting up and running a corporation.

Incorporation should not be an automatic step, because it may or may not make sense for you and your business.

Your Choices If You're the Only Owner

This section helps you decide what form of business to choose if you're going it alone: sole proprietorship or solely owned corporation.

Sole proprietorship

If you decide to carry on business as a sole proprietor (your business is then called a sole proprietorship), no legal distinction between you and your business exists:

- The property of the business belongs to you.
- The debts and liabilities of the business belong to you — you can be forced to use your personal, nonbusiness, assets to pay the debts of your business.
- The profits of your business are personal income and are taxed at your personal tax rate, and many

business losses can be deducted from your personal income.

How to set up a sole proprietorship

You don't have to do very much to set up a sole proprietorship. In fact, if you start doing business all by yourself right this very minute, without taking any further steps, you are a sole proprietor. Because it happens automatically, sole proprietorship is a very easy and inexpensive form of business to set up. You don't need the help of a lawyer. In most provinces you have to register your business name with the provincial government, but that's just about the only formal requirement you'll have.

How to run a sole proprietorship

No formal requirements about how to run a sole proprietorship exist. You can make it up as you go along. However, your accountant will probably tell you to set up a separate business bank account and keep track of your business income and expenses separately from your personal income and expenses — even though there's legally no difference between your personal and business income and expenses. Separating the two will make it easier for you to prepare the statement of income and expenses that, as a sole proprietor, you have to file as part of your income tax return.

The advantages and disadvantages
of a sole proprietorship

 The advantages of a sole proprietorship are

- Simplicity of setting up and running the business.
- Low cost of setting up and running the business.
- A tax advantage if your business is losing money — you can deduct its losses from your other income.
- A tax advantage if your business profits are low — the rate of tax you pay on your business income will also be low.

The disadvantages of a sole proprietorship are

- The income of the business is taxable at personal rates, which go higher than corporate rates. If your business does really well, and your income is higher than $127,000, then the tax rate can be as high as 54 percent.
- Your personal assets can be seized to pay the debts of your business, if the business can't pay them.

A solely owned corporation

If you decide to incorporate, you'll be the only shareholder of the corporation and the only director. But a corporation with only one shareholder or director is still a corporation. You have to follow all the usual steps to incorporate, organize, and run your corporation.

The incorporation process for a solely owned corporation is the same as for any corporation. You don't have to do anything extra, and you can't leave anything out, either.

Even though your corporation is just you, you must still fulfill all the requirements for director's and shareholder's meetings and resolutions. You can either meet with yourself over drinks, or simply make all your director's and shareholder's resolutions in writing. Unless you're really conflicted, you shouldn't have any trouble getting unanimous approval for anything you propose.

Other Legal Requirements

Other start-up concerns include topics like permits and licences, payroll taxes, getting a business number, and registering for the Goods and Services Tax (GST) or Harmonized Sales Tax (HST).

Permits, licences, and other government requirements

The odds are very good that some regulatory scheme — federal, provincial, or municipal (often more than one) — applies to your type of business. If that's the case, you may have to get government permission in the form of a permit or licence to carry on your business. The process for getting that permission may be short and simple (and maybe even inexpensive), or it may be long and complicated (and very expensive). But if you need government permission and operate your business without it, you may face a fine or risk having your business shut down.

You can find out whether your business requires permission to operate by consulting a lawyer, reaching out to a trade or industry association, or contacting the different levels of government directly. You can start by using the permits and licences search feature on the Canada Business website (www. canadabusiness.ca).

Payroll taxes and GST or HST

Without going into all the gory details here, if your business will have employees, you'll have to deduct and remit payroll taxes, and if your annual sales and revenues are more than $30,000, you'll have to collect GST or HST from your customers and pay it to the government. In other words, for most small-business owners, the requirement to charge/collect GST/HST doesn't apply until you've reached $30,000 in sales revenue.

Federal payroll taxes

Employers must withhold from their employees, and send to the federal government, a certain amount on account of the employees' income taxes, as well as the employees' contributions for Canada Pension Plan (CPP) and Employment Insurance (EI). Employers must also make CPP and EI contributions on behalf of their employees.

GST and HST

Briefly, the GST is a tax charged by the federal government on almost all goods and services supplied in Canada. GST is charged to everyone along the production and sale chain from the supplier of the materials, through to the manufacturer, wholesaler, retailer, and consumer. (Credits and refunds are built into the system to make sure that the government keeps only the tax paid by the ultimate consumer.)

Provinces that combine their provincial sales taxes with the GST charge an HST. Aside from Quebec, British Columbia, Manitoba, and Saskatchewan, all other provinces (except Alberta) levy the HST. The province of Alberta and the Northwest Territories, Nunavut, and the Yukon have no provincial sales tax, so only GST is charged. The Government of Canada website (www.canadabusiness.ca) has links to the exact tax rates charged in each province.

Any business that provides GST-taxable goods or services and has annual sales and revenues of more than $30,000 must register for, collect, and send GST or HST to the federal government. If your business's annual sales and revenues are less than $30,000, you don't have to register and charge GST, but you may do so if you want. If you don't register, you can't claim a refund of any GST you pay. Even if you expect your sales to be less than $30,000 for the foreseeable future, you might want to register for the GST so that your customers don't know that your business income is so low.

Your business number

If your business will be collecting and remitting GST to the government and/or collecting and remitting federal payroll taxes, you must register the business with the CRA and get a business number. The CRA uses this number to keep track of you, and you'll put it on your invoices to show customers and clients that you're entitled to charge GST or HST (and aren't just pocketing the money).

The Concept of Working from Home

There's no doubt about it — working from home is the cheapest way to go. With computers, high-quality multifunction printers, email, fax, and voice mail, a home-based business doesn't have to look like an amateur operation. And the Internet allows even the smallest company to have worldwide exposure. You can project a big business image even if your head office is the kitchen table.

 In addition to cost, working from home has other advantages, too:

- You'll be able to claim an income tax deduction for a portion of the expenses of running your home, even though you would have to pay these expenses anyway.
- You won't have the cost, irritation, and wasted time involved in commuting to and from work.
- You'll have more flexibility to deal with your children, aging parents, or pets.

Working from home does have some disadvantages as well, though:

- You may have little, if any, room for expansion as your business grows.
- You may find it hard to accommodate employees.
- You may find that you need facilities and services that you can't have at home.
- You may feel isolated from business associates.

• You may find yourself not isolated enough from family and friends.

But you can overcome most of these disadvantages (see the later section "Tips for working at home successfully"), so if possible, you should operate your business from home, at least in the beginning.

Should you have a home-based business?

It may or may not be wise, or even possible, for you to run your business from home, depending on

- The amount of space your business will need
- The type of business you'll be running
- The legal restrictions you may face
- The insurance you may need and your ability to get it
- The demands of your family
- The nature of your personality

Space considerations

How much space will the necessary equipment take up? Will you be able to fit your business into your home and still have a home to live in? If not, are you willing to let your business take over your home so that you're actually living in your office? If you need more space than you actually have to run your business, a home operation may not be possible for you.

Do you need to hire employees to help you run your business? If so, do your municipality's bylaws permit you to do so? And do you have enough room for employees and their equipment — not only enough to satisfy you, but enough to satisfy any provincial occupational health and safety requirements? Even if you go around with a measuring tape and determine that you physically have room for everyone, how will you feel about sharing your home with your employees?

The nature of your business

 Does the type of business you'll be operating lend itself to a home-based location? The answer is probably no if

- Your business requires a lot of heavy equipment — your home probably lacks the necessary infrastructure, such as reinforced floors, special ventilation or electrical capacity, to run the equipment.

- Your business is dangerous in any way — for example, if it produces toxic fumes or waste, or uses dangerous substances or equipment.

- Your business relies on a walk-in trade — because let's face it, you're not going to have high-volume pedestrian traffic on a residential street or down the corridor of your apartment building.

- Your business involves frequent meetings on the premises with clients who expect you to have professional office space. On the other hand, working out of your home is quite feasible if your business field is so informal that a home office meets your clients' expectations. A home office is also fine if your clients don't come to you at all — you call on them.

Legal restrictions

Before you decide to set up shop in your home, make sure that no legal reasons will make operating your business from home difficult or impossible:

- If you live in rented premises, check to see whether your lease prohibits you from running a business in your home.

- If you live in a condominium, find out whether the condominium bylaws forbid home-based businesses.

- Even if you own your own home, municipal bylaws may limit your ability to work from home. Investigate whether your municipality prohibits some or all kinds of business operations in your area; or prohibits employees; or requires a permit before you can run a business from your home.

Many landlords, condominiums, and municipalities turn a blind eye to in-home businesses unless someone complains. Maybe you can't imagine that anyone would complain, but your neighbours will get testy if your business brings extra traffic to the area, or creates noise or smells.

Insurance considerations

Don't assume that your home insurance policy will automatically cover your home business. You will almost certainly need to make changes to your insurance coverage and limits to adequately protect your business, so be sure to contact your insurance company or agent. You may even have to switch insurance companies, because some companies won't provide home insurance if a business is carried on in the home.

You may invalidate your home insurance policy if you don't advise your insurance company about your home-based business. Find out more about insurance later in this chapter.

Family considerations

Your family and friends may think that because you're working from home, you're not really working at all:

- Your children may barge into your office at will, whether or not you're on the phone or meeting with clients. Or perhaps they'll be capable of understanding that you aren't to be interrupted while dealing with others, but they won't allow you to complete so much as a thought if you appear to be alone.

- Your spouse may believe that you can now deal with every home repair, school meeting, or children's medical appointment. Your siblings may believe that you can manage any crisis involving your aging parents. Your pets may believe that you're ready and willing to provide treats and entertainment all day long. After all, because you're at home, you must have lots of free time — in fact you're probably looking for things to do so you won't be bored.

- Your friends and relations and neighbours may think you're now available for babysitting, dog-sitting, and other neighbourly chores, or are free to chat on the phone at any time of the day.

Do you have the moral fibre to set boundaries? Will you be able to tell your family, friends, and neighbours — firmly — that your work is important and that you aren't available to them during your working hours?

If boundary-setting doesn't work too well and family, pets, and friends bother you no matter what you say to them (and how loudly you say it), do you have the discipline not to be distracted by the interruptions?

Personality considerations

Perhaps you don't need outside interruptions, because you can interrupt yourself without any help from others. Of course, if you have a tremendous talent for being distracted, you can be thrown off task even when working in a stern and quiet office with a boss hovering over you like a drone, but your home has so many more fun things to distract you — the television, the refrigerator, even cleaning the bathroom if you're trying to avoid a particularly unpleasant piece of work. Getting on task and staying there takes discipline.

Or perhaps you're the opposite personality type. Getting down to work is not your problem; getting away from work is. You would stay at your desk 24 hours a day, 7 days a week, 365 days a year if you could. When you work in an office with other people, sooner or later they'll make you go home . . . if only to take a shower and change your clothes. When you're already home, no one will throw you out, so you must be able to limit your work hours on your own.

Even if you have the discipline to work by yourself without working yourself to death, think about how you'll like working without having any colleagues around. Will you feel isolated? Are you likely to stay in your pajamas all day and stop combing your hair? You'll have to make sure that you get out regularly and maintain contact with the outside world (see the next section for some helpful hints). Still, you have to be able to stand a certain amount of solitude to work at home.

Tips for working at home successfully

The following sections provide some tips for working at home successfully.

Keep your business separate from your family

Have a space in your home that is dedicated to your business, whether it's the basement, the attic, a spare bedroom, or a corner of your dining room. Use it only for working. That way your family will know (and so will you) that when you're in your workspace you're no longer "home"; you're at work.

If your workspace has a door, keep it closed when you're at work.

If your kids aren't old enough to be left alone, or disciplined enough to leave you alone, think about hiring a babysitter, at least part-time. Use that babysitter time to make your business phone calls.

Keep your business phone separate from your family phone

Unless you live alone, have a separate business telephone number if at all possible. That way, you won't have to worry about sullen teenagers rudely answering your business calls or taking messages that have about as much chance of reaching you as a message in a bottle tossed into the sea.

Get voice-mail service from the telephone company to make sure that your clients can leave a message for you if you're not there. Make sure that the outgoing message your clients will hear is professional in tone and updated daily. And be certain to pick up and return your messages promptly.

If you're on the Internet constantly and you don't have high-speed Internet service, consider getting at least one additional line, so that your clients can always get through to you on the phone. Call-answer is useful, but if you're in your office, clients will prefer to reach you in person.

Run your business like a business

Just because you're running your business from home doesn't mean it shouldn't be a professional operation:

- Don't be lazy, cut corners, or take shortcuts. Make sure that you comply with all legal requirements for your business and that you have proper insurance and all the equipment you need.

- Have appropriate stationery and business cards. Make sure that your business correspondence is neat, spelled properly, and grammatically correct.

- Be organized. Keep track of your appointments and deadlines. Have a proper filing system so that you don't lose important documents.

- Keep your work in the office and your food in your kitchen so that you don't have to worry about grease stains on your correspondence or coffee spills on your computer keyboard.

Have set work hours (even if they're odd hours)

One reason to work at home is so that you can be flexible in your work hours. But you should still have set hours. And if you're someone who tries to avoid working, setting fixed work hours will help you make sure that you actually do work. If you're a workaholic, setting fixed work hours will make sure that you don't work all the time.

Having regular business hours makes it easier for your clients to find you. If you must go out during your set hours, make sure that your call-answer service is set to take messages, and that you check for and return your calls promptly when you get back.

To reinforce the sense that you're "at work," dress in your work clothes during your business day. And be sure to take normal breaks, including lunch.

Create a comfortable working environment

Don't run a sweatshop. Treat yourself as well as an employer would in creating your work environment. Get a comfortable chair. Make sure that you have a large enough work surface. If you use a computer, make sure that the keyboard is properly positioned so that you avoid wrist injuries, and that you have a computer monitor that is easy on your eyes. Make sure you have adequate lighting and proper ventilation. Have plants, put up pictures, and play pleasant music (unless, of course, you hate plants, pictures, and music).

Avoid social isolation

Take advantage of being at home to spend some time with your family during the workday. Make a point of going out for lunch with friends or colleagues or customers or clients at least once a week. Get out of the house for a bit every day, even if it's just for a walk.

 A number of home business associations, many of them local, are out there. Join one, attend meetings, and take advantage of their information sharing and networking opportunities.

Don't lose touch with your field

It's important to stay current in your field and to make and maintain professional connections. Join a trade association or professional organization. Also, consider joining a local business association or attending events sponsored by your local chamber of commerce or board of trade if you have one. Subscribe to at least one trade publication. Use the Internet to check in regularly on relevant websites. Stay current with developments in your field by attending trade shows, conventions, and conferences, and by taking professional development courses in your field.

Make use of outside business support services

 Your business may need facilities and services that you can't have in your home, but that doesn't mean you can't have them at all. A wide variety of business support services are available, such as the following:

- Printing and photocopying services
- Couriers
- Packing and shipping services
- Research materials (at libraries or through the Internet)
- "Corporate identity" services to answer your phone calls and give you a business mailing address on a major street while forwarding your mail to your actual location
- Office centres that rent out office and/or meeting space on a part-time or occasional basis
- Freelance help such as secretaries and bookkeepers who work from their own business premises
- Virtual assistants who provide administrative, creative, and/or technical services on a contractual basis from their own business premises

Don't annoy your neighbours

Even if your municipality, landlord, or condominium association doesn't want you running a business out of your home, they're not likely to do anything about it unless someone complains. So, don't give your neighbours any reason to complain. Don't make too much noise. Don't let litter escape from your premises. Don't stink up the neighbourhood. Make sure that your clients or customers don't arrive at your door at odd hours or block your neighbours' driveways or park in their parking spots.

Know when it's time for your business to leave home

A home office is a great way to start your business. And depending on the nature of your business, it may grow in revenue without ever outgrowing the space you have in your home. But look for signs that it may be time for your business to leave home and get its own place.

The Use of Real Business Premises

If you can't work from your home, you'll have to look for business premises elsewhere.

Premises available, apply within

Different types of premises are available, and the type you choose will primarily depend on the nature of your business and where your customers typically work and live:

- **Retail:** If your business involves selling directly to the public, you need retail space. You can find retail space in a variety of locations, such as indoor shopping centres, outdoor strip malls, freestanding buildings, airports, train stations, hotel lobbies, office buildings, university campuses, and theatres. You may also be able to set up a retail operation in an industrial plaza (see the third point in this list).

- **Office:** You can find office space in downtown or local office buildings, business parks, above stores on streets with retail character, or in suburban shopping malls.

- **Industrial:** If your business involves manufacturing or large-scale distributing, you'll need industrial space for your manufacturing plant or warehouse facility. Industrial parks or plazas are zoned by municipalities to offer space designed for light manufacturing operations and for businesses that need showrooms as well as manufacturing facilities.

Space-sharing arrangements

If you can't work from home, it doesn't mean that you have to rent and equip your own retail store, suite of offices, or industrial space. You have other options for premises that may be of modest size, and cheap to rent and equip, and that may be available on a short-term basis. One of these arrangements may be right for you:

- If you need office space, you may be able to sublet a single office from another business, or rent an office in a business centre or executive suite — the landlord provides reception services and use of a boardroom and office equipment (as part of your monthly rent) and access to secretarial and other support services (usually for an additional fee).

- If you need retail space, you may be able to operate from a booth or cart in a shopping mall or in a pedestrian area. If your goods are seasonal, this may allow you to operate on a seasonal basis. A booth is also a good way to test your product before investing in a traditional store.

- If you need industrial space, you may be able to use a self-storage unit for your warehousing needs and maybe even for some light manufacturing or assembly of merchandise.

If you need space for your business, you should see if a business incubator is right for you. These mentoring facilities usually provide flexible rental space and flexible leases for start-up businesses accepted into their programs. See Chapter 2 for more information about business incubators and accelerators.

When you look for shared space, make sure that the premises meet the needs of your business. Find out the following information:

- **What the premises will cost up front:** Besides the first month's rent, will you have to pay last month's rent or a damage deposit?

- **What the premises will cost on an ongoing basis:** Will you be paying a flat monthly rental fee that includes all utilities and services, or will you pay extra charges for secretarial, reception, or cleaning services?

- **What access will you have to the space:** Will you be able to get into and out of your premises whenever you want to?

- **What limitations are placed on your use of the premises:** Will you be able to carry on all the necessary activities of your business?

- **What kind of security is available:** Will you be safe when you're on the premises and will your premises be safe against break-ins when you're not?

After you finalize arrangements for the space, you'll be entering into a contract. Make sure that the contract is in writing, that you understand it, and that it sets out all the terms that are important to you.

Insurance: How to Transfer Your Risks to Somebody Else

You can't eliminate every possible risk, even if you try. So, you also need to pass at least some of your risks off to somebody else. Who's going to be stupid enough to take over your risks? In case you hadn't already guessed, an insurance company.

Although you likely already know how the insurance process works, the fundamental point is that when you take out an insurance policy, you're in effect transferring the risk of financial loss or other horrible outcome (like the time and financial cost of a lawsuit) to another entity. You are not transferring the pain and anger of going through a fire or flood or, worse, loss of life. In the world of risk management, insurance is a key mitigation, and it's crucial. If nothing happens, the insurance company gets to keep its money — the premium that you paid to buy the policy. This is the best outcome.

Do you already have insurance?

You may think you already have enough insurance to cover your business, but you probably don't. For example, if you're going to run your business out of your home, your home insurance probably doesn't cover your business. Most home insurance policies exclude or limit coverage for business activities. If you're going to use your car as a business delivery vehicle, your existing car insurance probably doesn't cover that kind of business use. Key people in your business may already have life insurance — but the beneficiary is unlikely to be your business: It's probably their family members or their estate.

Do you really need insurance?

Some businesses need certain kinds of insurance, whether they want it or not, because they're required to be insured under legislation governing their field or under a contract they've entered into. (Commercial leases typically require the tenant to have insurance.)

But if you aren't required to have insurance, do you need it anyway? You don't need insurance against *every* risk. But insuring against certain risks makes a lot of sense. Take these examples:

- If your business involves giving advice, you should have insurance against giving bad advice.

- If your business involves manufacturing a product, you should have insurance against defective products.
- If your business involves having customers or clients come onto your premises, you should have insurance against injuries that occur there.

Having insurance protects you from going out of business if you're sued and the court rules against you. And it also ensures that anyone you injure receives compensation for the damage you've caused.

For risks that are unlikely to materialize or that won't cause big losses, you can consider self-insuring. That means bearing the risk yourself. Sometimes a risk is so remote, or the loss is so small, that you're throwing away money taking out insurance against it. You're also self-insuring in a way if you choose a high insurance deductible. Until your loss is higher than the deductible amount of your policy, you can't make a claim. (A higher deductible means a lower premium.)

You need to talk to an insurance agent or broker (agents work for just one company; brokers deal with several companies) about your business's needs. An agent or broker will help you evaluate the risks in your business and suggest what insurance coverage you need and in what amount. It's critical that you begin by knowing what perils (risks) you and your business face and, after that, which ones are insurable and to what extent.

Choose someone who is knowledgeable about your kind of business. Ask business associates for recommendations, and then make an appointment to talk to two or three of the agents or brokers recommended, before choosing one who seems best able to give you advice and find the coverage you need. Make sure the one you choose has errors and omissions insurance, as well as directors and officers insurance if you have a duly constituted board of directors. Errors and omissions insurance protects you if you make a costly mistake and damages result. Directors and officers insurance provides coverage for defence costs and damages (awards and settlements) stemming from wrongful act allegations and lawsuits against a board of directors and/or its officers. Then, if the agent or broker makes a mistake in getting the right coverage, you'll be able to recover compensation for any damage you suffer as a result.

 You may need different insurance from year to year, so you should review your coverage annually with your agent or broker.

Different Insurance Policies

Various kinds of insurance policies are available. You can often get a package policy geared to your particular kind of business. For a home-based business, you may be able to get a home business insurance package that provides coverage for things such as your business property (inventory, samples, supplies, filing cabinets, computers and software, tools, customers' goods) on and off the premises, loss of cash, business interruption if your home is uninhabitable, and legal liability (for products or services, or business-related accidents on the premises). Alternatively, you may be able to get an extension of your existing home insurance policy to cover your business. You may also be able to find packages for retail businesses, skilled trades, manufacturing, day care, or office-based businesses.

Here are the standard forms of insurance protection for damage by your business to others.

Liability insurance

Liability insurance, also called general liability insurance, covers your business if the *negligence* (carelessness) of a person in the business causes injury to a customer, client, consumer, or innocent bystander. This kind of insurance will pay the cost of defending a lawsuit brought against your business and will pay the judgment awarded by a court or the settlement negotiated with the injured party. You may be used to thinking of insurance as a fund that pays something to you if you run into trouble. The usual rule with liability insurance, however, is that payments go to the injured party, not to you or your business.

Commercial general liability insurance can provide coverage for a range of problems — for example, physical injury, property damage, and financial loss and liability under a contract. Some policies may also cover civil wrongs *(torts)* like libel and slander (collectively known as *defamation*) and false imprisonment. A commercial insurance package might also cover some of the following things, or you might have to arrange separate coverage for each:

- **Product liability insurance:** Covers third parties who are injured or suffer a loss because of a defect in a product you manufacture.

- **Errors and omissions insurance:** Covers third parties who suffer loss and injury caused by your careless advice or careless work.

- **Boiler insurance:** Covers ancillary damages caused by pressure vessel (pipe) explosions or malfunctions.

- **Tenant's liability:** Covers loss and injury caused by your business to other tenants of the building your business is in. If you rent commercial premises, be sure to show the lease to your agent or broker, to make sure you get all the coverage you're required to have under the terms of the lease.

- **Limited pollution liability:** Covers loss and injury to third parties caused by an unexpected or unintentional discharge of pollutants from your business.

 Automobile insurance covers loss and injury to third parties caused by your business's vehicles. This is not normally included in general commercial policies and has to be arranged separately.

Surety bonds, performance bonds, and guarantee bonds

Instead of getting insurance for liability you might have under a contract, you might be able to take out (through an insurance company) a bond that will be paid to the other party to the contract if you don't perform your obligations under the contract. (Bonds are commonly used in the construction industry.)

Fidelity bonds

You may want to have employees bonded (through an insurance company or a bonding company) if your business involves handling valuable property or working in other people's homes. If a bonded employee steals from a customer who makes a legal claim against the business, the bonding company compensates the business if the claim is successful. (A fidelity bond will also compensate the business if the employee steals from the business itself.)

8

Making a Marketing Buzz

Marketing is about creating — and then keeping — a relationship with your customers or clients. Whether you use traditional marketing methods or web-based marketing methods — and you should use both — marketing is about locating potential customers or clients or helping them to locate you, and then selling your product or service to them.

A Website of Your Own

Entire books have been written about business websites, and we only touch on some of the main points in this section.

The importance of a website

Should your business have a website? In a word, yes. Setting up your business website is the first step in establishing and maintaining a presence on the web.

Your business should have a website because

- **It lends credibility to your business.** People expect certain things of a business — a phone number, email address, fax number, and maybe even a street address. And more and more, people expect a business to have a website; if it doesn't, potential customers may wonder whether you're really serious about being in business!

- **It lets the world know you're there.** You don't have to do business through your website, but potential customers like to be able to look up information without having to call you during business hours. Virtually all Canadians are now connected to the Internet or have ready access to it, and many of them begin their research about businesses not in the Yellow Pages, but on the web. A website is a great way to describe your products and/or services, hours of business, location (including directions and a map if you'd like), and contact information such as phone and fax numbers and your email address.

 All kinds of other tools called *widgets* can be added on as well. Widgets are special apps that can be added to a website to provide extra functionality, including booking calendars, advertisements, weather information, or links to your social media pages. To make sure that your website appears prominently on search results, check out Google's advertising tools at `https://ads.google.com`.

- **It provides service to your existing customers.** You can post answers to your customers' or clients' frequently asked questions (FAQs), allowing them to get answers on their own whenever they want. An online FAQs page can save you time in dealing with simple, repetitive questions. Your website can also provide a point of email contact for your customers, especially if, for some reason, you don't want to give out your email address to every passing stranger.

You can have a "contact us" section on the email that allows customers to write to you without your actually having to show your email address. Thus, you can avoid being spammed by everyone.

- **It allows you to carry on your business.** You can use your website to actually sell your goods and services to the world, 24 hours a day, seven days a week.

A server of your own versus a web host

No one will be able to find your website unless you have a *web server*, a computer that is connected to the Internet 24/7 and delivers (or serves up) web pages. Any computer can be turned into a web server by installing server software. The web server stores all the files needed to display the pages of your website when someone connects to your site using a web browser.

Many web server software applications are available, such as Internet Information Services (IIS), available for purchase from Microsoft (www.microsoft.com), and Apache HTTP Server, available free of charge from the Apache Software Foundation (www.apache.org). Of course, you'll still need an Internet service provider (ISP) to connect your web server to the Internet.

Does all this sound too technical for you? If you don't have the technical expertise, and you don't want your own web server, you can use a *web host*, a business that provides space on its server. You can check with your ISP like Rogers, Shaw, Bell, Videotron, and many others to see if it offers an appropriate monthly hosting package (you'll likely be entitled to some free web space as part of your existing Internet package). You can also find web hosting services by searching the web for *web hosting*. Your choice of web host will affect which software you use to create your web pages, and may affect your web address and the appearance of your site.

One of Canada's technology success stories is Shopify (`www.shopify.ca`). Shopify is an end-to-end online e-commerce platform that lets you start, grow, and run a business. With Shopify, you can create an online store or an online representation of your physical

store. You can sell in multiple marketing channels, including web, social media, online marketplaces, mobile devices, and physical shops. The platform has functionality to let you manage products, inventory, payments, and shipping. Shopify is completely cloud-based and hosted, so you don't need to maintaining software or computer servers.

Your domain name

The first step to setting up a website is to register your own domain name or uniform resource locator (URL). When you register a domain name, you're inserting an entry into a directory of all the domain names and their corresponding computers on the Internet.

The basics of domain names

A domain name has two parts. The first part identifies the site's name, and comes before the dot. The second part, which comes after the dot, is the top-level domain — one of the primary categories into which Internet addresses are divided. The most common top-level domain name is `.com`. In Canada, a website may use the country code top-level domain name `.ca`.

The Internet's Domain Name System (DNS) allows a website to use a domain name instead of a long, complicated string of numbers (which is what an Internet Protocol [IP] address is). The DNS is administered by the Internet Corporation for Assigned Names and Numbers (ICANN), an internationally organized, nonprofit corporation that oversees the distribution of domain names.

 You have to be a little more special to register a domain name ending with `.ca` than with `.com`. You must meet certain Canadian presence requirements. For example, you must be

- A Canadian citizen
- A permanent resident of Canada
- A legally recognized Canadian organization
- A foreign resident of Canada who holds a registered Canadian trademark

How to choose a domain name

You have to come up with a unique domain name — if possible, your domain name should be the same as the name of your business. Check whether your name is going to be the same as, or confusingly similar to, another business's trademark or name or trade name by entering your potential domain name as a web search.

If someone is already using the domain name you want, you may be able to buy it from the owner. Check for contact information on the owner's website or try to contact the owner by typing in the domain name at www.register.com/whois.rcmx or https://cira.ca/ca-domains/whois. You can also find websites where people offer to sell their domain names (www.sedo.com or www.register.com).

Domain name registration

After you've decided on a domain name, you can register the name by buying it through a registrar. Check the ICANN website (www.icann.org) for a list of ICANN-accredited registrars and their web addresses, or, if you're interested in a name ending in .ca, the website of the Canadian Internet Registration Authority (CIRA; www.cira.ca) for a CIRA-certified registrar. You can also arrange to buy a domain name through a web-hosting company or an ISP that provides hosting services. The transaction is completed online and will include a search to ensure that the name you want is available to buy.

When you buy a domain name, you're actually getting a subscription to use that name for a set period of time, usually from one to ten years. Your domain registrar will send you a reminder 30 to 45 days before the subscription runs out, but if you don't renew it within 60 days, the name may be released to the public.

 Make sure that your domain registrar has your most up-to-date email contact address so that the renewal notice doesn't disappear into cyberspace.

Your website's content and design

After you have a domain name, you have to put some content at the web address — and that becomes your website.

Content

No matter what your business, every business website should contain certain things:

- A description of your products and/or services, including your background and areas of expertise.
- Your hours of business and, if you have a physical business and want people to come to it in person, your location (including directions and a Google Map).
- Contact information such as your address, phone and fax numbers, and email address (or if not an email address, a contact form).
- Information that new and existing customers will find useful and that adds value to your website and your

business, such as FAQs about your business or service or products (and of course some intelligent answers), a blog, informative and/or how-to articles, and links to other helpful websites and to your Facebook and Twitter pages (find out a lot more about these later in this chapter).

- A link to allow visitors to your website to sign up for your email newsletter.

- A Terms of Use Agreement containing a website information disclaimer regarding the accuracy of the information contained on your site, as well as a copyright notice claiming copyright in the content of the website. In Canada, a copyright notice isn't actually necessary to obtain copyright protection, but it might make web surfers think twice before pilfering your content.

Also include your privacy policy, if your site collects any personal information from your customers, as well as a hyperlink disclaimer, if your site contains links to other websites, stating that you don't guarantee or endorse the linked sites.

If you sell goods or services on your website, your Terms of Use Agreement should set out the terms of your usual contract for the sale of goods or provision of services, as the case may be.

Design

After you know what you want to say on your website, make sure to say it. You may find the prospect of designing your own website a bit overwhelming, but getting help is easy. WYSIWYG (short for *what you see is what you get*) website creation software takes you through the process step-by-step without your having to know HTML coding.

You can also find businesses that will help you design and set up a website. For a basic website, you can expect to pay from $500 to $1,500. Search the web to find a web designer whose portfolio (and price range) appeals to you, or get business acquaintances to recommend their website designers.

Many ISPs offer help with the entire process from domain name selection through web hosting (check out Hostpapa at www.hostpapa.ca) to website creation (which firms like GoDaddy Canada at http://ca.godaddy.com can help you with as well).

The design of your website should suit your business. If you're setting up an accounting firm, you want your site to look conservative to show you're responsible with other people's money. If you're running a rent-a-clown business, you might want to have a little livelier splash and colour. Whatever the look of your site, it should be

- **Fast:** Your web pages should load quickly, so keep the bandwidth-hungry bells and whistles to a minimum.

- **Legible:** Use easy-to-read fonts and make sure that your text and background are in contrasting colours. For example, don't use navy blue text on a black background, or pale pink text on a white background.

- **Understandable:** Your written content should be clear and concise.

- **Secure:** If your site collects any personal information from your customers, especially credit card information, your site must use technology that encrypts (or encodes) your customers' information. Secure Socket Layer (SSL) or Transport Layer Security (TLS) technology are the most commonly used. You must also comply with the privacy provisions of Canada's Personal Information Protection and Electronic Documents Act (PIPEDA).

How to attract visitors

Many of your potential customers will do a web search to find businesses that offer products or services such as yours. Make sure that your business will show up in the search results of the major search engines such as Google, Yahoo!, and Bing.

Getting your website listed with a search engine is only a start. You also want to try to get it ranked as highly as possible in the search engine results — this is called *search engine optimization* (SEO). You can do this by identifying the keywords that people will most likely use in a web search for your type of business, and repeat those words frequently on your home page. You can also use a paid SEO service such as Search Engine People (www.searchenginepeople.com) or AddMe (www.addme.com).

You can list your website with individual search engines by going to the search engine's website. You'll be asked to submit your URL — your domain name — and information about your business. If you don't want to do the work yourself, you can use a free submission service such as AddMe (www.addme.com).

The Use of Social Media to Market Your Business

The term *social media* is used to describe online media that allows readers or viewers to participate in the creation or development of the content — in contrast with traditional media, which merely delivers content. Traffic on social networking sites such as Facebook, Twitter, and LinkedIn has grown dramatically over the last decade.

Should you be using social media to market your business? Proponents of social media marketing say yes. Some studies suggest that consumers are more likely to buy from businesses they come into contact with through social networking sites.

On the other hand, opposing studies suggest that social media isn't as effective a marketing tool as many people may think. Detractors blame the influx of fake news and *trolls* (crusty people who only post negative comments) over the last few years. Many entrepreneurs surveyed in these studies found that social media marketing required more effort than they anticipated.

The following sections tell you a bit about some of the top social networking sites to help you decide whether social media marketing is for you.

The major social media sites

In 2019, the top three social networking sites in the United States and Canada were Facebook, Twitter, and LinkedIn, according to Small Business TRENDS (www.smallbiztrends.com), as well as many other Internet analytics companies. You probably don't have time to participate in all of them, and even the most ardent supporters of social media marketing recommend that you limit yourself to two or three sites — but which ones? You want to use the sites your customers use, so ask your customers which social media sites they frequent, and join those.

The following sections look at the major social media sites that will be the most useful to you as a small business owner.

Facebook

Founded in 2004, Facebook has more than 1.5 billion monthly active users. This makes it one of the best forums for connecting people with your business. Start using Facebook by creating a fan page for your business. Unlike a personal Facebook profile, fan pages can be seen by everybody on the Internet. You can do this free of charge by going to www.facebook.com. Facebook's extensive Help Center (www.facebook.com/help) provides general information about using Facebook, as well as information about business solutions.

Any Facebook user who visits your fan page will see the information you post. Facebook users can choose to become fans of your page by clicking the Like button on your page. Then, any time you post content on your fan page, the content will also show up on your fans' pages, where, in turn, their Facebook friends will see it.

Encourage customers, clients, and colleagues — even family and friends — to become fans of your page. You should also promote your page on your website, in your email newsletters, and in your print materials.

After you have your page, you can use it to post information, photos, and videos, as well as links to other websites. Fill your Facebook page with new content on an ongoing basis.

 For some ideas on content, search on Facebook for the fan pages of your competitors and see what they're doing.

Unlike a blog, where you have the choice of whether to allow comments by your readers, the essence of Facebook is community and participation. So, at least some of your posts should encourage discussion among your fans.

A Facebook page is an ongoing commitment. You have to monitor the discussions and come up with new content on a regular basis.

Twitter

Twitter was founded in 2006 and has more than 320 million active monthly users. Many users use the 280-character limit to pass on information. Businesses can use Twitter to interact with potential clients, answer customer questions, release the latest product news, and use targeted advertising with specific audiences.

As you likely already know, Twitter is a micro-blog platform that allows its members to post short messages — *tweets* — containing no more than 280 characters. As long as a member's Twitter account is set to public status, anyone, member or nonmember, can view that person's Twitter page. Members can choose to "follow" other members on Twitter. Whenever a member posts on Twitter, his or her tweets automatically go out to all of his or her followers.

You can sign up for a Twitter account free of charge at www. twitter.com. Be sure to sign up in the name of your business. After you sign up, visit the Help Centre and have a look at the Twitter Basics section. Search to see if your competitors have Twitter accounts, and if so, check to see how they're using Twitter in their businesses. Do this by using the Find People link on your home page.

Twitter also has a search function (http://search.twitter.com) that you can use to search your business name to see if you appear in anyone's tweets. And if so, you should consider responding. Do this by starting your tweet with the person's username preceded by the at symbol (@).

Encourage your customers, clients, colleagues, family, and friends to follow you on Twitter. Promote your Twitter account on your website, in your email newsletters, and in any of your printed materials.

What will you tweet about? You can, for example, tweet

- Links to stories about your business
- That you've updated your blog, and provide a link to your blog
- About sales, events, or loyalty programs

Be sure to check your Twitter account regularly to see if your customers or clients have tweeted to you. If they have, be sure to respond.

Twitter can also be a great tool for finding potential customers. Use the Twitter search function (http://search.twitter.com) to search keywords that describe your product or service. Perhaps someone out there is looking for the very product or service you have to offer.

LinkedIn

Launched in 2003, LinkedIn is the most popular social media site for professional individual networking. The website is available in more than 25 languages and has well over 400 million registered users. LinkedIn is ideal for people looking to connect with other people in the same industries or sectors, networking with local professionals, and displaying business-related information and statistics. LinkedIn is more business oriented than most other social networking sites. LinkedIn's motto is "Relationships Matter" and its stated mission is "to connect the world's professionals to make them more productive and successful."

Join LinkedIn for free at www.linkedin.com. The Customer Support Center (www.linkedin.com/help) provides answers to frequently asked questions.

You can join LinkedIn as an individual and create a profile summarizing your own accomplishments and areas of expertise. As a member, you can then develop and maintain a list of people you know and trust in business — called *connections.* LinkedIn members can connect only through *invitations.* You have to invite the other person, who must then accept the invitation. If the person you invite to connect is not already on LinkedIn, he or she will have to join in order to accept your invitation.

Your business can also have its own profile. After you establish a business profile, people searching for businesses in specific fields can find it. You can ask other members to give you a *recommendation* that you can include in your profile.

After you join LinkedIn, search for customers and suppliers and connect with them. You should also search for your competitors to see if and how they're using the service. And search to see if any *groups* (smaller networks based on type of connection or area of interest) exist that are relevant to your business and expertise, and ask to join. You can then participate in the groups' discussions and demonstrate your knowledge and expertise to other group members.

Instagram and your business story

This section tells you about Instagram, a Facebook-owned company. Hundreds of millions of people are using Instagram, so for that reason, as well as the reality that a picture really is worth a thousand words, you should consider leveraging this unique platform for your business. Instagram is suited for any size of business, and it can make your business come to life in the minds and eyes of potential and existing customers.

Like Twitter and Facebook, you can partner with influencers and use creative hashtags that can increase your visibility and better engage with customers and clients. Instagram is ideally suited to mobile devices, so that makes it a particularly stable and convenient platform to use in business.

The following sections highlight some of the more important aspects of Instagram that you need to be mindful of.

How to set up an Instagram account

When you've decided to use Instagram, and as you begin to set up an Instagram for Business account, make sure that your username on Instagram matches the username of your other business social media profiles. It sounds obvious, but many businesses fail to do this and miss out on the ability to *go viral* (have a friend tell another friend about your product, service, or idea, and so on). Aside from this element, the only other information that appears on your public Instagram profile is your website address — which you can readily update to promote campaigns or new pieces of content on a new page — and a short bio.

Instagram is all about images and image, so your Instagram profile photo should be your company's business logo to make it more discoverable. Discoverability is also enhanced because people who follow you on Twitter or Facebook will more readily recognize your brand.

After you've set things up, kick off your Instagram presence by following a bunch of users. Think about customers, significant influencers in your industry sector, and other people in the ecosystem of your business. Add your Instagram handle to your website, as well as other social media profiles, for cross-promotion.

How to align content with your business strategy

Your marketing and communication strategy, to the extent that it's also using Instagram, should address what your business hopes to achieve by using Instagram. For example, a new business will want to efficiently and economically attract customers and build brand awareness and value, resulting in increased sales and raw traffic to your website. Instagram is well suited to enhancing this type of initial and ongoing engagement. It can help you generate these and other attractive business outcomes.

How to develop a content strategy

Your marketing and communication strategy should be underpinned by pictorial content that makes sense. Wedding photos may be perfect for a post that stays posted for, say, a decade. But for a fast-moving and ever-changing business, you need to constantly refresh your images. Ideally, a posting schedule that makes the most sense is one that considers variety and freshness but stays clear of daily carpet bombings of your followers with endless images.

 Be sure to keep your content style consistent as you proceed with updated posts and even a variety of business themes. However, as much as possible use the same color filter or hue for every post in order to create a unique style that will be recognized by your followers.

Be careful how and when your business engages on Instagram with other accounts on Instagram — this includes everything from liking and commenting on other people's photos to professionally and personally dealing with the incoming comments on your own account. Also, consider the best way to use nonvisual text elements within your Instagram posts. For example, it's best to use common language or style for captions and a brand-oriented hashtag descriptive of your business.

Check out mobile photo-editing apps like Enhance or VSCO for filtering and editing your images and importing them into Instagram.

Time to get creative

A golden rule of marketing is to grab some positive attention. One way to do this is to combine a reasonably sized and mixed collection of photos and videos (Instagram currently allows up to ten per post). Remember that captions are critical — they present an excellent opportunity for you to tell a story about your business. Captions let you expand on the image and give it some context.

Also, Instagram Stories, a feature on Instagram where you can capture and post related images and videos in a slide-show format along with text and drawings, has more than 240 million average daily users. Do you need to know more? It can pay to get to know Instagram's extra features.

How to get even fancier and more technical

Instagram has recently launched special tools for business users. These tools include new business profiles, analytics, and the ability to create ads from posts directly within the Instagram app.

If you have a business profile you can choose how you want your customers to get in touch with you. They can call, email, or text your business with a tap of a contact button, and they can get directions to your location as well.

Insights on Instagram is a feature that provides businesses with useful information about who their followers are and which posts are more effective than others. This feature lets you identify top posts, reach, and the extent of user engagement around posts, as well as privacy-respecting data on your followers like gender, age, and location. Learning about the behavior and demographics of your target market is always a good idea. Instagram also lets you convert well-performing posts into ads right within the Instagram app. To create and run an ad, you'll be able to identify your most popular and existing posts on Instagram and then add a button or icon to encourage potential customers to take action.

Management of your social media marketing time

So, now you're pumped and ready to use social media to market your business, and you've decided to use Facebook, Twitter, LinkedIn, and Instagram. Hmmm. How long will this all take? Log in and post on Facebook. Log in and post on Twitter. Log in and post on LinkedIn. Assuming you're also maintaining a blog on your website and creating and distributing email newsletters, how will you have any time to carry on your business — even if you recycle your content?

Help is available. Check out HootSuite, a for-fee service (www.hootsuite.com). It supports anywhere from 10 to 35 social media profiles. A final point about social media is that you don't need to leverage this marketing and outreach channel if your existing or potential customers don't use social media. However, trends are definitely in your favour if you do leverage it, because more and more Canadian small businesses and individuals are jumping on this online bandwagon.

About the Authors

Andrew Dagys is a Chartered Professional Accountant and risk management expert. As a best-selling author, he has written and co-authored more than a dozen books, mostly about investing, personal finance, business, and technology. Andrew has contributed columns to major Canadian publications. He is a frequently quoted author in many of Canada's daily news publications, including *The Globe and Mail,* the *National Post,* and the *Toronto Star.* He has appeared on several national news broadcasts to offer his insights on various current events and topics. Andrew considers writing books, and collaborating with talented publishing partners, to be one of life's most truly amazing experiences.

Margaret Kerr and **JoAnn Kurtz** are lawyers and entrepreneurs — and they have the bumps, bruises, and scars to prove it. Occasionally, they find a minute of free time here and there, which is how they came to be the authors of, among other books, *Buying, Owning and Selling a Home in Canada* (now in its second edition); *Canadian Tort Law in a Nutshell* (with Laurence Olivo, also in its second edition); *Legal Research: Step by Step* (with Arlene Blatt, another one in its second edition!); *Make It Legal: What Every Canadian Entrepreneur Needs to Know About the Law;* and *Facing a Death in the Family.*